GARDENS

GARDENS

HOLLY PRADO

HARCOURT BRACE JOVANOVICH, PUBLISHERS
SAN DIEGO NEW YORK LONDON

"Born under a Bad Sign" lyrics and music
by Booker T. Jones and William Bell.
© 1967, 1970 by East/Memphis Music Corp.
Copyright assigned to Irving Music, Inc. (BMI), 1982.
Grateful acknowledgment is given to E.P. Dutton for permission
to reprint an excerpt from *Justine* by Lawrence Durrell.
Extract from "Shaking" reprinted from *The Streets Inside:
Ten Los Angeles Poets*, Momentum Press, 1978.

LIBRARY OF CONGRESS CATALOGING IN PUBLICATION DATA

Prado, Holly.
Gardens.

I. Title.
PS3566.R24G3   1985   813'.54   85-8703
ISBN 0-15-134291-1

Designed by Michael Farmer
Printed in the United States of America
First edition
A B C D E

This book is for Harry E. Northup.
Love sustains work.

With thanks to those creative writers
who have supported me—financially and artistically—
in the writing workshops that I teach.
Without their belief in their own creative work,
my work couldn't exist.

The angels of Silverlake and Echo Park helped.

NOTE

A novel is an interior map, not an exterior one. Los Angeles, as it appears in this novel, is a mix of people and places—some actual, some not. Whatever I've moved and shifted in order to write *Gardens*, I'm sure that Los Angeles, possibly the most imaginative city in the world, will understand. I hope the reader will understand, too, and accept the myth and the outer reality as a whole, as fictional truth.

GARDENS

1

"I HATE TO SEE THINGS DIE." Kate, alone on the porch, leans over the arm of her rocking chair, settles her empty iced-tea glass on the floor and picks up a jacaranda blossom lined with tiny veins. By tomorrow, in this heat, its lavender will have faded to greasy ocher. "The tree can't hold such a burden of flowers," she thinks. "They're all over the porch and yard." In May, she loved this great show of color, but she can't stand the shedding, though she knows the tree will bloom again next year.

She stretches, then falls back into the old basket of a chair she's pulled out from the house. "Fierce weather. After all my years here, I'm still not used to Los Angeles. The desert heat. The sudden brush fires and those winter downpours that take away what's left of the burned-off hills." She drops the jacaranda blossom, her fingers sticky with its oil. "But it is a gorgeous city." On the other side of the yard, star jasmine bushes never tire of putting out white spirals of odor for her imagination to dote on at night.

She hears her daughter, Sheila, move toward the porch. Maybe she hears Sheila's familiar walk. Maybe nothing, really. Maybe her hair—the tangle of brown curls racing along her neck and shoulders as a signal that she can't wait for something to happen. "Twenty-two years old. I couldn't wait, either."

"There's no such thing as security," Alex had said fifteen years ago when they bought this house. One of his aphorisms. They haven't believed that owning a particular piece of property will save them from anything. "But," Kate confesses, flapping her work shirt to stir a little air, "I have come to depend on this sprawling place." The house is in Silverlake, a neighborhood closer to Mexico than to Hollywood. Its light, livelier than anywhere else in the city, invites creative people and blurs status. Kate looks across the street at the comforting mélange. The Horseleys' caramel stucco house boasts a romantic, if unwieldy, balcony stuck to the front stone facade. Next door, a white bungalow has a trellis overwhelmed with scarlet bougainvillea. The Watanabes' mustard yellow cottage is circled by a jade green fence, and its red tile roof shows splotches of yellow where the housepainter slipped. Farther down the block, the houses seem, to Kate, like knuckles of a hand, unalterably attached to the street, to her sense of home.

This home. Sheila called it "the house with the windows" when they moved in. She had spent her first few years in cheap apartments with windows that stuck in

2

their frames, and for her this house was a fairy tale—two stories and an attic and a big backyard with a lemon tree, a fig tree, another jacaranda and plenty of room for a garden. Under the trees, there are canvas lawn chairs that Kate and Alex and Sheila, and sometimes even Audrey, Kate's mother, like to lounge in to watch the sunset and toss out peanuts to the blue jays that swoop down in the early evening.

A wooden something-or-other stands at the end of the backyard. They call it the greenhouse, and it is painted green—probably used, years ago, for gardening tools, seedlings, general clutter. They use the service porch off the kitchen for all that but don't tear down the shack, which was Sheila's playhouse when she was little. Alex likes the earthy smell of it. Audrey refers to the place as "that eyesore," but Kate defends it as a historical treasure, laughing, saying she could grow orchids there.

They've tried to keep things open. They kept the windows open—all of them—and the doors, too, until five years or so ago when break-ins started in the neighborhood. "We've had a messy, tender life that began as a rebellion against Audrey's stiff living room. Now, it's simply our life." Kate smoothes loose hair from her sweaty forehead and tucks it inside the rubber band that holds the rest behind her neck. "Our life, which is about to change." There's change in the jacaranda tree. In Kate's recent paintings. In Sheila. Sheila's face has filled with California sun as Kate's never has. Kate squints into the glaring afternoon light, her own face thin-skinned, as fragile as the jacaranda flowers that shudder in a fist of breeze that shoves across the porch.

3

On an otherwise simple night when Sheila was ten, she locked her bedroom door for the first time. Kate wanted to give her the ritual good night kiss that she hoped would keep her child alive until the next morning.

"It's Mom," she whispered through the door.

"I'm going to fall asleep by myself tonight," Sheila whispered back.

Kate tried the door, felt unexpected pain, nausea as if she'd sprained an ankle or cracked a knee.

She had five hundred sketches of Sheila in the garage, which Alex had remodeled for Kate to work in, though there hadn't been time for serious painting when Sheila was first born, not while Kate was absorbed with nursing and diapers, and later with first days of school, then with piano lessons that convinced Kate of Sheila's gifts. There wasn't enough time while Kate was completely in love with her only child. Still, she sketched: Sheila asleep; Sheila giggling over a stuffed Winnie-the-Pooh. Sheila at the much-too-large baby grand piano, one of Audrey's indulgences. Sheila writing her early stories about magic deer in a forest like Griffith Park, where Kate and Sheila often went for walks. Five hundred sketches in ten years, some in spidery pencil, some in charcoal, others in pastels—all useless talismans against a child's growing up. Sweating on the porch, Kate thinks, "Sheila doesn't belong to me. None of us belongs to anyone. But don't we? Somehow?"

Alex had followed Kate to the garage that night and said, "She's not dead, you know." But Kate began to tear up the sketches one by one. After the first few, she stopped, asked for a drink. Alex brought the whole bottle of scotch.

They sat on the cement floor drinking, looking at Sheila, Sheila, Sheila. Finally, Alex gathered the sketches and put them back in the makeshift racks he'd set up for Kate. Then the two of them lay flat on the floor, holding hands. "All right, she's not dead," Kate admitted, although her stomach still ached.

Audrey was in a rage when Kate told her over the phone about Sheila's locking herself in. "You're encouraging her to be just like you!" she shouted. "You're letting her be an introverted nut!"

Kate pushes loose hair into the rubber band again, then rubs at her tense neck. She feels other hands. Sheila has come through the open front door to stand behind her, to massage steadily with her long hands—the hands of all those piano lessons, full of music. But now she wants to be a writer.

"I'm glad you're home for the summer," Kate says.

Sheila plans to go back in the fall to San Francisco State, where there are good writers in the M.F.A. program. She's just gotten her B.A. but isn't sure she's graduated from anything. Her world seems old or used or silly. She's been pawing through her records every day, searching for music she really wants to listen to. Not Keith Jarrett and not Joni Mitchell. Not Laura Nyro, who can usually be counted on. It's not even Beethoven, although the "Ode to Joy" of the Ninth Symphony has always been her response to confusion.

She's been stumbling over things in the house. That wonderful antique desk with treacherous claw feet in Alex's study. The kitchen chairs around the oak table. This morning in her room, she knocked over a whole shelf of records. As they skimmed across the floor, she muttered, watching Laura Nyro wheel on top of Beethoven, "I can't be in this house anymore."

"Listen," she says to Kate.

"Rub that thick muscle over to the right, would you?"

"Listen. I need to leave." Sheila feels the muscle tighten. "Loosen up," she says, then plunges into the speech she's been saying to herself most of the afternoon. "Mac knows about an apartment I can sublet for a couple of months. It's cheap—well, cheapish—and if you could let me have the rent, I could eat with Mac most of the time—hey, I'd always come to see you and Alex, too, but—" She's been leaving for years. Has left. Hasn't left. "I can't seem to get it together here."

Kate's afternoon solitude becomes loneliness, and loneliness becomes helpless mounds of flowers scattered over the porch. "Can't you stay home? It's July. You've only got until mid-September." She lifts Sheila's hands off her neck and holds them in front of her. Musky tan, not Kate's moon white skin. "Sheila, my mirror and my stranger," Kate thinks.

Sheila jerks away to perch on the railing. Her skin is copper in the sun. Her heavy, clove brown hair masses around her shoulders, curling tightly in the heat. She crosses her legs and swings the top one energetically. She recounts everything her mother has ever believed about independence.

Kate listens, rocking, and finally says, "You're right. I have a life of my own with my painting. I'm a serious painter to myself and to a few others, which frees you from the worry that I'll rattle around the house with nothing to do. And, yes, Alex and I are still very much married. You've never had to suffer the breakup of your family, and there's no reason to think you ever will. That saves you the burden of divorced parents, getting grumpier as they get older, demanding your attention. Yes, yes, I've always said you should be who you want to be. Audrey did make me miserable. You've been raised with joy. I've wanted you to be as vital as you are—"

"You just can't let me go, can you?"

"Of course I can." In three of Kate's recent paintings, there are figures that lean to each other, yearning. The paintings are red. Deep blood. "But not this summer, okay?"

Sheila pushes herself off the porch railing. Kate hears her banging up the inside stairs, imagines her as she's seen her so often—plunked on her bed with three pillows behind her, a looseleaf notebook—her journal—open in front of her, writing intensely with the special fountain pen that no one could buy for her. She'd foraged through every stationery store in Echo Park and Silverlake until she found the marbled green pen that fit her hand perfectly.

The afternoon deepens but doesn't cool off. Sheila can write out her anger. Kate wants some kind of prayer. Nothing comes to her in the formal, reassuring words of the King James Bible, the language she's heard inside herself since Sunday School days in the Midwest. Psalms, laments, parables. She stops rocking, gets up. The work shirt sticks to her. Pulling it away from her back, she steps through the jacaranda blossoms into the house. Instead of a prayer, she thinks of Marc Chagall's paintings based on "The Song of Songs." A young woman, tranquil, asleep in her pink tree. Another canvas of merging lovers, peaceful deer. A dove flies. A hand reaches. She says, out loud, the words belonging to the painting, "I am my beloved's."

"Forgive yourself," Alex says, after Kate burns the last batch of garlic bread, forgetting it under the broiler. Sheila says, "Mac and I have to go anyway." Mac finishes his fourth slice of cold roast beef, which Alex earlier urged Kate to cut in thick slices: "We really can afford it now," making her laugh at her propensity for artistic poverty, artistic thrift, thin artistic slices of rare roast beef.

Sheila says she may or may not be home. Alex and Kate aren't to worry. They have Mac's phone number, which is where she'll be if she doesn't come home. Should she call? Oh, it's not necessary. Well, maybe. Yes, if she's going to be at Mac's, call and let them know. Mac gets up from the round oak table, shakes Alex's hand enthusiastically, kisses Kate on the cheek, says, "I'm going to get some great photos tonight. We're heading for Venice to a poetry reading Sheila's hot to get in on."

"The cold soup was terrific," Sheila says in Kate's direction as she gets up and takes Mac's hand. "Just enough chopped chives and dill and all those things you put in it. Thanks for feeding us."

As Kate dumps the burned bread in the trash, she hears the click of the front door, then silence. People leaving her. Alex collects the soup bowls, plates, silverware, runs soapy water in the sink. She's grateful for the words "Forgive yourself." She thinks of Sheila and the scene on the porch, which she described to Alex when he came home from his committee meeting. He didn't comment, just stood with her in the kitchen and watched her cut the roast beef, urging, "Thicker, Kate! Thicker slices!" so she could laugh. Then Mac arrived, and Sheila came downstairs, beautiful, her hair freshly washed. Kate, on impulse, said that of course she and Mac should have dinner here— why spend money for nothing but atmosphere on a Friday night in a crowded restaurant?

Who were the poets Sheila wanted to read last Christmas? Sylvia Plath. Adrienne Rich. Names Kate had heard vaguely sometime or other but had to search out in the bookstore up on Vermont Avenue—W. C. W.'s, after William Carlos Williams.

Almost eight o'clock now. Not quite dark. July, with its late light, its heat, the feeling it gives Kate that she's exposed, always being photographed the way Mac will photograph those Venice poets tonight. Venice—a romantic's scheme for creating a village with Italian canals. The water in the canals is grimy these days; the village houses are shadowed by high rises and high rents. There's tension in the mix of wealthy professionals, poor blacks and Latinos, poets and gurus. Roller skaters career along Ocean Front Walk every weekend, where vendors sell mechanical toys, print dresses from India, shish kebab on a stick. The last time Kate was there, she couldn't hear the ocean, only a few yards away, for all the street musicians. Yet the music was sweet. A black woman and her Texas-cowboy-looking husband, longtime Venice characters, sang the blues, sugared by the woman's experienced voice.

Kate sits at the table and watches Alex's hands move from plate to plate, soaping and rinsing. He has to lean far over the sink. She's always startled by his height because his movements are compact and quick. Although his legs seem too long for his torso, he balances himself with an ease Kate sees as charm. He can charm her into laughing at herself. He's charmed work and money from a wild assortment of people in and around art. He lures the blue jays with peanuts in the backyard better than anyone else.

The dishes are stacked to drain. He says, "Let's go out for ice cream."

Kate doesn't want to go anywhere.

"Rocky road," he says.

"I'm too full."

"Boysenberry ripple."

"Aren't you tired? You worked all day."

"Yeah, but I'm willing." He nuzzles her ear. "Vanilla pistachio almond cherry banana fudge."

"Let's relax."

They leave the kitchen, move to the living room, tell each other how strong the moon is just beyond the big south window. It's almost full, isn't it? They nudge the couch around to face the window and sit for awhile, giving themselves up to the rising moon, cool as fresh water tonight. Alex unbuttons his shirt. Kate takes off her sandals. The hardwood floor under her feet feels fine, firm and packed like earth. "You can feel the energy from the old Indian power places around the neighborhood." So Alex takes off his Birkenstocks, those special sandals he wears. Kate unbuttons her shirt, still the work shirt, one of Alex's that she wears for luck when she paints.

Upstairs, they sit on their bed. The relief of night air

edges through the window next to the bed, and Kate opens the window wide, sees the moon again, certain of itself, taking its time. Alex has gotten out the tin oolong tea box printed with Chinese flowers that holds their stash of marijuana. Kate likes watching his hands as they pick out the seeds and crush the grass until it's just right. His hands are a painter's hands, although they haven't done a painting in years.

"I'm not Picasso," he said one day a few months after Sheila was born. He was holding the baby, drying her with a towel after her bath while Kate sketched. Flatly: "I'm not Picasso."

His long neck bends over the tin lid of the box, which he uses as a tray to roll the joint. His hair is the rich brown of Sheila's, full, but graying. Kate supposes that if she did a portrait of him now, it would just be a lot of hair and hands. "Forgive yourself," he had said, about the garlic bread, about her scene with Sheila. "Forgiveness comes at the end of something," she tells him. "We're not at the end."

"Maybe we are." He lights the joint, and they pass it back and forth. "Sheila makes me nervous. All that hair." He blinks against the smoke as Kate hands the joint to him. "I don't think I can have her around much longer." He inhales deeply.

Grass makes Kate mute. They sit without talking until they finish the joint, until Sheila is far away in Venice, until the moon has passed the window and they're both buzzing and smiling. Kate reaches for Alex. He reaches, too, to kiss her throat and her breasts under the unbuttoned shirt.

11

Hours later, Kate wakes up. Sheila can go. She should go. Kate lies still. In the dark, she knows the shape of clothes on the floor: her shirt and khaki shorts, Alex's jeans. She knows what's inside every drawer of the dresser, on each hanger in the closet. Yet Alex said he didn't want Sheila around. He didn't give a real reason. Can he let her go so easily? "I don't see everything," she realizes, not even everything in the room. She can't say who wrote all the letters they've kept, who's in the photographs, which of them remembers a birthday as a wound or a blessing. She can't name what Alex is dreaming as he nods in his sleep. Saying yes to a dream woman? Or to the ghost of his rabbi grandfather?

"Darkness." She whispers the word. Such mysterious reds in her three recent paintings. In the fourth, which she's working on now, is an old, old woman. Maybe. Sometimes it seems to be Audrey. Staring into the shadows on the ceiling, Kate finds a vague face—undefined, haunting. Alex stirs. She feels his dreaming shift. Who accompanies him in his sleep? Who is with Kate? She stares at the shadows until there's no pattern at all, only subtle shades of darkness.

Audrey and Kate came to Los Angeles in 1947 from Albion, Michigan, a college town where the Methodist foundations of the college were mirrored in the sturdy brick dormitories and chapel and classroom buildings, even in the town's shops and houses. Kate's father owned a drugstore, one with a soda fountain that was a note of pleasure on a cautious Main Street. Roy filled prescriptions. Audrey mixed sodas, dispensed Green Rivers, cherry

12

Cokes. At thirty-two, she was lively and blond—"perky," in the 1940s jargon she used to describe herself. She daydreamed of full-skirted dance dresses like the ones Ginger Rogers swirled in.

Roy, at forty, thought Audrey was perky, too. He doted on Kate without making much fuss about it. A precise man who measured powders and capsules all day, he wasn't given to overstating, or even stating, his feelings. On a crisp fall morning, Roy left to open the store as usual. There was a smoky tang in the Michigan air—that anticipatory excitement of a season coming into its own, when the trees were their most vibrant and the town had filled with a new crop of college kids. He reminded Audrey that they'd better go over the books that night. When he saw her morning smile fade, he managed to give her a wink, then a quick kiss on her pink lipstick to lighten the idea of dull accounts after a ten hour day at the store.

After she had sent Kate off to school and mixed a meat loaf for dinner, Audrey walked the three blocks to the store. Her pink cotton uniform was new, but she thought she ought to buy a pair of decent shoes. Her feet ached from yesterday's long hours behind the soda fountain. Audrey's people were farmers in Kansas. She'd never minded hard work but had had something a little different in mind when she married Roy—something different in a new state, in a new town with the classy name of Albion. She stopped to lean against a maple tree for a minute to take off a black pump, the one that pinched the worst. The clean, medicinal scent of the store revived her as she walked in. Then she saw Roy. He was sprawled on the floor near the prescription counter, dead of a heart attack.

Audrey and Kate didn't stay in Albion two weeks after Roy's funeral. Roy's attorney, who had an office above the drugstore, took over the business—gallon bottles of Coke syrup and all. The sale gave Audrey enough money to leave Albion, ship the little furniture she had, buy new clothes. They were on a train heading for Los Angeles before either of them could think about saying long good-byes—goodbye, for Kate, to the first twelve years of her life, to the peaceful small town where the clean river was within walking distance of anyplace.

The train pulled out faster than Kate thought it would. She waved to her dearest friend, Rosemary Collins, who'd skipped school to come to the station and smile and smile. Rosemary was gritting her teeth to keep the smile going so she wouldn't show how bad she felt that she and Kate weren't going to take walks along the river again, talking about who was cute and who wasn't in the sixth grade. Through the smudged window of the train, Rosemary's face was grotesque. The smile and the teeth jerked crazily as the train picked up speed.

Kate started to cry when she couldn't see Rosemary anymore and could hardly see Albion, either—just the spire of the college chapel sticking up through autumn trees. She thought of her favorite hymn, "Follow the Gleam," and cried harder, her tears splotching her new sweater, a special wheat-colored one Audrey had bought especially to match Kate's hair. Audrey got out her handkerchief and brushed at the sweater where Kate's tears dampened it. She told her they were on a grand adventure. Didn't Kate want to look as pretty as she could for Los Angeles?

14

Their "new life"—Audrey's phrase—was too new for Kate. She'd never seen a palm tree. They lined the streets as if they had some business there, but Kate couldn't imagine any use for them. There were no low branches to climb and no true leaves. No part turned crimson or gold in autumn. When hard winds funneled through the streets, palm fronds would fall, dangerously sharp and heavy. Kate had never heard anything called a frond, a word that escaped her from time to time. She'd think, "Palm leaf," but knew that wasn't right. She'd search her mind until she found "frond." The shift from maples to palms, from brick to stucco, took a long time. Staring at the pink Spanish-style apartments like the one Audrey had rented made Kate feel she was playacting. Saying the word "frond" over and over made her feel the same way. Words like that were an act. The Methodist college was real. The smell of disinfectant on the drugstore counter was real.

She went to libraries. They were familiar, at least, and quiet. She needed quiet, although she couldn't have said why. But her body was both empty and weighted with all she'd left in Albion. In libraries, everyone talked softly, a bit stiffly, which suited her fine. She liked pictures that stood still. Roy had subscribed to magazines, the *Saturday Evening Post* and *Collier's*, big magazines with big pictures. Kate always headed for the art section of the downtown public library on Hope Street. "Hope"—that was easy to say. Whenever she said it, she'd see that library, solid, sitting there at the end of Hope Street with enough art books to take care of her for years.

She liked the library and she could bear the ocean. The

15

ocean was constant and patient, though startlingly powerful. On Sunday afternoons, Audrey and Kate and a few of Audrey's friends, other typists from the West Coast Sportswear office, would go to the beach, whatever the weather. Although Audrey had gotten some checks from the attorney in Albion, there had also been debts. She hadn't stayed unemployed for long.

The friends were new to L.A., too, and ready to be swept off their high-heeled feet by the exotic. They'd drive along Wilshire Boulevard all the way to Santa Monica, or along Sunset just to see the palms and citrus trees, admire actual lemons growing right there in front of them. "Even at Christmas time!" one of them would invariably say. Lemons in December. Anything could happen. These grown-up ladies, Vinnie and Flo and Helene, would bring Kate gifts: sample vials of cologne, tiny candy store boxes with four plump chocolates in them, a fresh hibiscus blossom. Flo would pin the flower in Kate's hair with two crossed bobby pins and say, "There! A real Dorothy Lamour."

Flo was Jewish and had a car—a 1939 Chevrolet, beige. She would give Kate rides on the running board if they were going very, very slowly in or out of a driveway. Flo was the only Jew whom Kate and Audrey had ever known. She was also the only person Kate had met who was divorced. The car was a legacy from her husband. "A good man," Flo would say, "but useless, if you know what I mean, when it comes to knowing what a woman needs when she needs it." This was followed by a great, collective sigh from the other women in the car until someone pointed to a particularly impressive row of palms, thirty feet high, lining the street. Then the sigh became quick gasps of pleasure.

Kate would eat a chocolate covered cherry from the little candy box, taking one bite first, then sucking out the sugary cherry juice, then eating the rest in two quick bites, but munching the cherry, the surprise, for as long as she could. She liked surprises if they were sweet. She liked it the day she came home from school and found Audrey there, home early, with a brightly wrapped present.

"No special occasion," she said with a grin, "just a present for my very best daughter."

Had Kate done well in school that term? Maybe she was, as Audrey said, simply a very best daughter, though Kate always thought she was supposed to earn that title. She did try for high marks in school. Late afternoons, she dusted Audrey's lamps and vacuumed because Audrey hated "little things on the carpet." She tried and kept trying, but it was already too late for either of them to change the other, to change fate, divine will, whatever caught Audrey in a vision of Los Angeles success, whatever caught Kate in a dream of hope—the place of silence and art.

Audrey was too vital to want to stay home, even if she could have managed it financially. But she was too old to start over, to erase Kate. The only child. The best daughter and the rebel, the opposite and the mirror image. The present was a brand-new copy of a book Kate had been checking out of the library over and over for months: *American Art after 1900.* She carried it to the ocean when the women went there. She'd sit on the sand—loving the

17

sea but afraid of the waves—while the women splashed in the surf, and turn repeatedly to the color plate of a black woman wearing a yellow dress, striding down a city street. Staring at the painting, Kate could see the woman walk and smile and talk mischievously to the men who sat on porches in the background. Kate liked that—men appreciating a woman so obviously appreciative of herself. Kate saw how she loved her yellow dress, silky around her legs. She would look at Kate and say, "Honey, there's lots of folks who'll talk you to death about being nice, but I'm sassy and proud." By the time Kate was fourteen, she knew she wanted to make a woman walk and tease and throw back her head and laugh—by painting her, curve by curve.

2

ALEX STANDS OVER KATE, holding out a mug of steaming coffee. He's already dressed in a loose gray shirt and lightweight cotton pants. She comes awake slowly, the gray blurring in front of her. "The owl," she thinks, wondering if this is 1957, the year they were married. She thought of him then as an owl—the wise bird with a secret understanding of life. He pushes the mug at her, urging her to wake up.

"Sheila didn't call last night," he says.

"She must be home then, don't you think?" She reaches for the coffee.

"I don't know. I didn't knock on her door."

"Were you afraid of seeing her or not seeing her?"

He doesn't answer but sits beside her on the bed, takes her mug, sips, hands it back to her. "I've got to go."

What time is it? Still cool—it can't be past seven. Good.

19

She wants to paint this morning. There used to be owls in the neighborhood. She hasn't heard one for a long time. "Where did the owls go?" she asks.

"Scared off to the park, I guess," he says, meaning Griffith Park with its miles of hills and trees. He sips again from her cup.

The coffee's just right this morning. When he makes it, he brews it from the utterly black blend they buy at the Latino market down on Sunset. It sits in its yellow can, striped with red, on a shelf next to jars of herbs that can start a menstrual period or cure a headache. This part of Sunset runs east through Silverlake and Echo Park, slides into downtown Los Angeles where it becomes Macy Street, then turns into Brooklyn Avenue and moves through East L.A., which really is Mexico. But a lot of Mexican Americans live in Echo Park, the neighborhood southeast of Silverlake. Echo Park and Silverlake lean on each other—Latinos and Anglos and Orientals and Jews and blacks leaning into a mix of colors and languages. Sunset leans against odd shops, old houses, graffitied walls, an occasional new shopping center featuring Japanese sushi to go or one hour film developing. All of this leans against the hills that keep the whole in place.

"There's still a stuffed owl over the meat counter at the Trails on Sunset and Echo Park Avenue," Kate says. "They took down the moose heads, though, when people began to get concerned about the environment."

"I've *got* to go."

"Knock on Sheila's door, will you?"

"You do it." He kisses at the top of her head, then leaves.

20

Kate, nude, gets out of bed, yawning. She's tall enough to see over most people's heads at a movie. She stretches to her full height for a minute, then relaxes. Morning. The darkness is gone from the room; the ceiling is unshadowed. It's cool, and she can get her work done early. She pauses. Too cool. Something unnaturally chilly in the room. Something about the stuffed owl, about how living things can disappear. "I'd better check on Sheila," she thinks, grabbing her robe and heading down the hall.

Knocking. "Just grunt. Let me know you're in there." Knocking. Knocking. Then she jiggles the doorknob; the door opens.

Sheila's room has windows that look north out over hills studded with houses the colors of summer squash, bananas, plums. Kate waits for the room to focus. She rarely comes here, even when Sheila's away at school. Once Sheila leaves for good, it will be a fine place to paint. The attic is stifling, even with two electric fans. In the winter, it's drafty. She appreciates the skylight and likes being removed from the rest of the house. But this room—broad, open, letting in the direct north light from the hills—will be great for painting. Sheila chose the room for herself when they moved in, but it isn't really hers, is it? It belongs to the house, and the house will still be here after Sheila leaves.

Sheila has picked up the records that fell yesterday. They sit in a pile on the floor. Several notebooks, her journals, are next to them, and next to the journals is the bed with Sheila in it. Her back is to Kate. She's pulled the sheet up to her neck, and it floats along her body with her breathing.

21

Kate waits until Sheila rolls over in bed toward her. She opens her eyes. "Mom?" A bruise intrudes on her forehead like a vicious bite.

"Sheila! What happened?" Kate hurries to the bed, pulls Sheila into her arms. Sheila slips her mussed-up head under Kate's chin, a child. "The bruise. What happened?"

"Nothing. Can I just sleep some more?"

"Sure. But give me a clue. What happened to your head?"

Sheila sits up, holding the sheet around herself. She looks out of the window closest to the bed, as she does every morning. Hills. Familiar houses. She touches her head as if she's testing something that might be too hot. Last night begins to work in her—the poets and the exciting talk afterward about writing. Pressing the bruise, she hears what one poet named Livia, who had a voice like an eggshell cracked on the side of a bowl, had written: "No directions for coming alive, but every shape throws its sparks." It was an accusation, as if Sheila with her new B.A. had bought directions. Ouch.

She decides to keep last night to herself until she can sort it out, so all she says is, "It hurts." She's whining. She hates to whine. Damn it. All right. An explanation. "Mac's car got rear ended on the way home. I bumped my head on the dashboard, hard, you know, harder than I thought."

"Is Mac okay?"

"Yeah, he's fine."

"You didn't stay at his apartment? You didn't huddle together and make passionate love to convince yourselves that everything was all right?" Kate feels as edgy as Sheila feels childish.

22

Sheila looks out at the hills again, steadies herself. "We hung out with people from the reading until really late. I didn't want to stay at Mac's, that's all. It wasn't a bad accident. The police didn't even come. Mac's bumper got a little crunched. I just didn't—"

What do you use for bruises? Heat? Ice? Didn't Sheila wear her seat belt? Were they drunk or stoned? The expression on Sheila's face is as bruised as the black and blue spot. Did somebody hit her? "Was it really an accident in the car?" Kate asks.

"I'm telling you the truth," Sheila hisses.

"It's ice; that's what you use for bruises," Kate thinks. "I'll get you some ice," she says.

"I'm not thirsty," Sheila moans, and lies down again.

The phone rings in the upstairs hall as Kate leaves the bedroom.

"Audrey Jones for Kate Levinsky," Audrey's secretary says.

"Hi, Midge, it's me."

"Hi, Kate. Hold on. Your mother wants to talk to you."

"Kate?"

"Hi, Audrey."

"Are you tied up for lunch?"

"I don't know. Sheila's—well, she's home, you know."

"Can you both have lunch with me? Can Alex come, too?"

"No, I'm sorry. He isn't here."

"Drinks? Late afternoon?"

"What are you doing in your office so early?"

"Working. What are you doing?"

"Waking up. Look, come over here about four, how's that?"

"Four? At your house? Let me think. All right. Fine, in fact."

"Is ice the best thing to put on a bruise?"

"Right. For a long time. Whose bruise?"

"Nobody's. Just asking."

"See you at four."

The ice, wrapped in a towel, is carried to Sheila. Then Kate goes to the attic where she turns on the two fans. Their whir cuts the gathering heat and also cuts off sounds. "Blessed whir," she thinks, shifting away from Sheila's bedroom, from her own bedroom and Alex, into the thrill she feels as she studies the painting that sits on her easel asking her to see what she's done so far.

As the work emerges, Kate learns it. She doesn't know what she paints as she paints it; it simply moves, a birth. Then there are long moments like this, staring at what has come forward, relishing the intensity she wasn't aware of as she worked, considering how each stroke fits—or doesn't—and what's to be done next. She puzzles over the various reds: blood, ripe fruit, the hibiscus Flo used to pin in her hair. None of this is obvious, but Kate sees it. Summer warmth. Autumn harvest: the red deepens in places on the canvas, ages into the single figure at the bottom which is there but not there at all. "The old woman?" she wonders. She can't tell. It's changed overnight. It's not Audrey; it's not anyone. She wants to paint the figure to see past her own ignorance of it. If it's not an old woman, who is it? If it is an old woman, why has she lost herself? The shape keeps its secret. "Don't insist," she warns herself.

"Palimpsest," she thinks. Layers of paint over layers of paint, land that's been farmed again and again. The figure will be painted like that, growing out of its own strange history. Memory on memory—personal memories and then others that are in the archetypal dreamworld that isn't anyone's alone. This painting belongs to Kate, yet doesn't— just as her family is and isn't hers.

Orange catches her eye in the background of the canvas, a small section she barely noticed herself painting yesterday. It isn't harsh sunlight, is lively but cool. She remembers mixing it with white and blue. There's still a little on her palette. She mixes more, fills the brush, touches it to the canvas. "Wow," she says. It's the orange she needs today, and she falls into the rhythm of painting without hearing the fans or smelling the drowsy old wood of the attic walls, without seeing anything but orange, a memory of how Silverlake light falls against the hills after it rains.

The other three paintings in her present series stand behind the easel. The first one shows a man and a woman with their backs to the viewer. The man's hand stretches to the woman's, but a bar of Kate's sharpest red burns between the hands. The man's other hand strains upward, although there's only emptiness above him. The figures are insubstantial, suggesting the absence of physical body. Kate thought, "Death," as she saw the painting develop, but the almost invisible fingers of the man's hand, reaching up, made her see Adam and a desire for God that can never be satisfied outside the Garden. She made numerous sketches of these people's faces, wanting names for their yearning, but never drew anything she could use. The faces would disappear into her paper before she could see features.

In the second painting, both the man and the woman

25

are in profile, reaching upward. Their reaching is directed to each other but also to the space beyond them. As they face one another, they do have mouths and noses, foreheads and cheekbones, but no eyes. The rest of their bodies is abstract, part of the reds, not separate from unconsciousness. Another shape, bulky and mysterious, fills the bottom of the canvas. At times, this third thing appears to be an ancestor, offering its hand, but there are many fingers on the hand, and they can be monstrous, snaking up to draw the struggling man and woman into chaos.

When Kate was painting the third figure, she would often feel it fill the attic with a presence like history, a supportive thickness. Other days, she'd find herself choking, as if it had her by the throat. The shifting reds of this creature keep the conflict of its nature—sustaining, then suddenly vicious. By the time she was through with the second painting, she thought the series was complete. Two companion pieces. She was startled when she came to the attic to work a few days later to find the same difficult reds moving onto a new canvas. She'd planned to fool around, do a couple of action paintings that didn't demand any preparation. But there were the reds, and gradually a third painting occurred in which the three figures stand together, much more developed, each with a face, with hands—many hands reaching for the others. It's impossible to tell whose hands are whose, but there's victory— a flame of understanding—in the specific yearning for one another, for union. This painting was done with a push of glorious energy that Kate was sure meant completion.

She had lain on the attic floor when she knew the third painting was finished and stared up through the skylight and thought about three, a number she'd considered when she and Alex, as art students in the '50s, spent time studying Jasper Johns's paintings of numbers. The shape of 3 fascinated her. It was somebody getting out of a chair, an ocean wave about to break, an ancient rune. She began to read about three and found that when there's tension between two things, its release can create a third, a unity that was unexpected in the tension itself. Kate, musing on this as she lay on the floor, was pleased. But in her reading, she'd also found that three lacked a fourth, that four was the numeral of wholeness. She groaned.

The fourth painting began with tentative sketches that didn't show any figures. "Where did they go?" she'd asked, curious about the disappearance of all that yearning. It wasn't until she set up a large canvas and really started to paint that the old woman—or whoever it is—appeared, as if she had been waiting for Kate to take her seriously.

Kate hears a sound behind the whir of fans. Faintly, "Mom?" Is it Sheila? Probably just the fans, just Kate's imagination, but it interrupts her fascination with orange for a minute. Kate used to ask Sheila to pose when she was thirteen. It was so brief, that moment between buds and breasts. Sheila wouldn't. She thought Kate was making fun of her. Everybody, she thought, was making fun of her.

At thirteen, Sheila spent hours on her bicycle, pedaling wildly around the neighborhood; then she'd come home to stare at herself in the mirror or drop helplessly on her bed and cry. She had a red skirt she wore when she started to menstruate—she wore it every month and would never

27

say why and didn't even know why herself. She'd turn in the full skirt so fast that it would make a circle, twirl until she was dizzy, until Alex and Kate noticed her, until she could excuse herself from the room because she was so dizzy and could run upstairs to flop on her bed and cry again. Because they'd noticed. Because they hadn't noticed enough. Because they'd said something. Because they'd said nothing.

Kate watched Sheila as if she were watching herself, moved by forces she didn't understand. In February of that year, 1971, she woke up one morning listening to what she thought were enemy planes, hundreds of planes, until Alex rolled over in bed toward her, then on top of her, and said, "Earthquake." He rolled them both to the middle of the bed, where they lay as if they'd been buried together. All Kate could think was, "Let it all stop."

Kate married Alex in 1957 to be with the artist he was, to be with herself as the artist he loved. Their child was the creation of two artists, of life lived with respect for beauty, high passion, study, artistic idealism. She believed they were wonderfully different from others and could protect themselves from turmoil. The '60s erupted to shatter that fantasy. Kate, a child of the '40s, discovered that the world wasn't progressing reasonably, logically. When they moved into this house and Alex said, "There's no such thing as security," she smiled. One of his owl statements. But not one, she thought, that would shake her as powerfully as it did.

For Kate, the mid-'60s were a revolution against quiet libraries: Flowers and sticks of incense appeared in Silverlake along with posters of Jimi Hendrix and Janis Joplin.

The stoned sensibility was colorful on the surface but disintegrated into chaos. A pointless war in Vietnam, ODs and deaths. Even now, Kate sometimes sees a young woman in the nearby streets who stays stoned all the time, stands in the middle of any sidewalk clutching a piece of ivy or a little flower to her head. Her jeans are unzipped so that her belly shows, and she thrusts her body forward—an incarnation of a time past. "Love me and I'll love you and it's love that will save the world." Universal love, stoned on its lost possibilities. The young woman gyrates and holds the bit of ivy to her head and grins, but can't talk if anyone stops to ask her a question.

Kate took mescaline just once. She cried all day. She wrote the only poem she'll ever write but couldn't decipher it the next afternoon and tossed it in the trash as Alex came home. He was earlier than usual. He shoved past her to the refrigerator, got a beer, took one big gulp, then poured the rest down the sink. He sat at the table but got up again right away to get another beer. He didn't make it to the refrigerator. At the sink, he turned to stare out the window, then down into the sink where the spilled beer was slowly leaking through the drain. "My God," he said, "Gene's dead."

Kate, shaky, still recovering from the mescaline, started to cry again, although she'd never liked Gene much—and never felt he liked her. He was stubborn and hard on people, hard on himself. They only had to look at each other for Kate to feel she ought to do more with her life. Gene was one of Alex's students at Gill Institute, where Kate and Alex had once studied art, where Alex frequently taught a couple of classes. Alex thought Gene gifted, invited him to the house once in a while to talk about emerging L.A. artists—about Billy Al Bengston's polymer-lacquer chevrons or the delicate pencil work of Ed Moses. Gene had the same wheaty hair as Kate. She recognized in him the stubbornness of her farm relatives. Once, he said, "When I'm an old geezer, I want to look at my body of work—all my paintings—and see that I've been alive every goddamn minute." Unlike most other art students, who had managed to dodge the draft, Gene enlisted for Vietnam. The army found him sharp-eyed and coordinated and tough and made him a helicopter pilot.

Kate pulled her poem out of the coffee grounds and melon rinds. She'd show it to Bob Hunt. He was a bridge, a comfort, more than simply a gallery owner who admired her work. He'd offered her a strange home among the paintings and assemblages and sculptures of better-known '60s artists. While Alex was hustling jobs, while Sheila was growing toward the night when she would lock her door for the first time, while Kate was wondering if she was any kind of artist at all, Bob met the '60s with aplomb. Maybe, in this crazy time, he'd have a sane word to say about an indecipherable poem, about Gene's terrible death in an impossible war. Bob, with his confidence, his way of holding Kate in his arms that made her feel momentarily complete, was something of the security she'd lost. But he was also a wrench away from her real home, part of the confusion that eventually led her to despair.

The '60s didn't end for Kate in 1970. When Sheila began to menstruate, to twirl in her red skirt, Kate felt even more dizzied than Sheila. After the 1971 earthquake, she tried to read philosophy. She ached for clean systems

30

of knowledge. Alex had picked up Sheila's adolescent moodiness, too. He leafed through Seventeen, admiring young models with pouty mouths. He fussed with his food. Conversations were ruined by either Alex's or Sheila's complaining, "Nobody understands anything!"

Kate was working in the garage. She began to paint white canvases that were all about ways to get out. Where? She thought the paintings would tell her, but they were only exits, not answers. White with freezing white with milk white with gray white.

Perfect philosophies rose in her head, but the clarity of Leibniz's "pre-established harmony" dissolved into white windows, alleys, stairways that were no more than cloudy holes. As the windows cracked from rectangles to disjointed, detached lines, Kate knew she was exhausted. Would she lose Alex to Seventeen? He'd gotten those part-time jobs teaching art classes at Gill. He'd written articles for Now Art magazine—was even assistant editor for a while. He did free-lance layouts for advertising agencies. He'd managed Bob's gallery at times when Bob wanted to go to Europe for two or three months. Alex was everywhere, seeing women with Sheila's body, getting a shiver of arousal from fresh mouths and sudden breasts. Kate was thirty-six, and there wouldn't be any more children. It wasn't only Alex's attractions that worried Kate, but her own. To Bob. To romantic chaos that Leibniz couldn't harmonize. What was a creative life, anyway? Her brush pounded at the white paintings until one autumn afternoon she couldn't stand any of it anymore.

She found herself in the kitchen staring at the calendar on the wall. It was one from Rolling Stone magazine with

31

pictures of anti-everything rock groups. "I could kill myself before Sheila and Alex get home," she thought. The
gas oven was three steps away. The white paintings were
out in the garage. No hope of rescue in them. She turned
the pages of the calendar month by month and saw the
date of the earthquake. She'd circled February 9 with a
red pen to remember. In April, she'd marked her birthday.
She turned to May, to June, to July, then flipped to September. The picture for the month was a man tattooing a
spider on the bare ass of a young woman. Should she kill
herself today, September 20, and circle the date?

She sat down at the oak table. The memories gathered
into a great weight: a dead helicopter pilot; Sheila's menstrual blood; Bob reading her mescaline poem and then
putting his arms around her without explaining anything.
The earthquake she'd heard as the enemy. In the middle
of that memory—the ground splitting and thundering—
she tried to stand up. She managed but couldn't move
from where she stood. Her thighs were strangers with
separate lives. Her hands were as large as her thighs and
couldn't reach for anything. She forced herself to recite a
poem she'd learned in elementary school about elves in a
British garden. When she was able to whisper the rhyme
all the way through, she could imagine herself her own
size. When she could finally move her hands to rest them
on the table, her knees crumbled and she had to sit down
again.

Then, suddenly, she grabbed the phone. She called five
or six women in a food co-op she'd joined and blithered
about organic carrots. One of the women had kids near
Sheila's age. Kate recounted a recent dramatic dinner scene

in which Sheila had deliberately poured sugar instead of Parmesan cheese on her spaghetti so she wouldn't have to eat it. She had developed a fierce aversion to tomato sauce. Sheila had wailed in artificial shock, then gone upstairs to cry. The woman laughed. She and Kate talked about taking a couple of weeks off and going to Mexico, which they never did, but they planned to bask on glorious stretches of deserted beach without being able to talk to or understand anybody. It helped.

Kate didn't cook dinner that night. She didn't cook for the next month. Alex or Sheila cooked, or they went out to eat. Kate didn't explain. Alex would lie next to her in bed, night after night, holding her. He'd fallen in love with Kate the first day he'd seen her in a crowded studio at Gill as she sloshed burnt sienna on her canvas. She was painting a still life setup of three eggplants with technical skill but no respect for actual color. He'd walked past her easel and with his own brush full of paint drawn a huge X across her work. "Never be bored with reality," he'd said.

Alex came from a family in which reality and imagination were painfully strained. His father, Sol, composed atonal music. "The music of objectivity, clarity," he insisted as he hovered over his piano. Reality was Schoenbergian theory: the future of great music. Sol's strident dissonances would be recognized as masterpieces. His wife and two daughters worked to pay the rent. The women were unreal shadows, allowed to glide along the walls of Sol's genius. Such a separation of the artistic and the practical struck Alex as disastrous. He went to art school to discover his own inner vision but also to find out how

33

to work in the world. Kate's irreverence angered him, but under his impulsive X he saw the precision with which she painted. She said evenly, "I think we'd better have a cup of coffee and talk." As he got to know her, he found that her combined Midwestern sense and imaginative strength were exactly what he was looking for in himself.

She would lie in bed that autumn of the white paintings, somehow betrayed. Alex hadn't given her much encouragement lately. He kept changing jobs, putting all his effort into making enough money to keep the house going and to save what he could for Sheila's college. He admitted that he was a little nuts, but if he flipped through the pages of girlish adolescence with Sheila's magazines, it was only an attempt to have some fun while he worked his ass off. Strawberry lips and short skirts were nothing.

"Windows," Alex said one day, coming into the garage, though Kate had warned him to stay away. He stroked her arm as if he were stroking a stray cat, looked at the white paintings around the garage. He sat on the floor as he had three years before when they'd spent the night with all those sketches of Sheila. He pulled Kate down to sit beside him. They both looked at what she'd been trying to get herself out of, the mess she'd gotten herself into. She twisted away from him, angry that she was being forced to give up her secret paintings to Alex. But he kept his hand on her arm and wouldn't let her stand up until they'd seen it all.

The next time Kate went to the garage, she discovered that she was out of white paint. She was usually attentive to supplies, but there just wasn't any more white. The paintings, she saw, were finished.

. . .

"Mom?" again. Kate silences one of the fans. "Mom?" Sheila is at the bottom of the stairway to the attic. "Can I come up or you come down or something?"

"Come up."

Sheila presses the towel full of ice cubes over her bruise. The ice is melting, dripping through the towel and down her cheeks. She eases into the one chair in the attic, near the easel. "How's the painting?"

"It's okay." One more delicate spot of orange. Kate puts down her brush and turns to Sheila, although she's not quite out of her painting yet.

"This may sound strange after yesterday," Sheila begins, "but I don't know where I want to be this summer." She leans back to rest her head, but the chair isn't high enough and the water from the ice pack runs down her face, so she sits up, wishing Kate would kneel next to her, pat her knee, offer comfort instead of that blank, waiting face. All right. Tell it all. "Last night, we heard these poets read. Their poetry was—oh, it was *real*. One poem Livia read—she's about my age and has this crackly voice that sounds like it's going to burst any minute into absolute truth—and it does—she read a poem about swimming—diving and almost drowning—but taking risks." She wipes a stream of water from her cheek. "Kate, these people live in L.A., and they work here and aren't in school. They have ideas—their own ideas, not somebody else's." Lifting the ice pack, Sheila checks the bruise. It's still swollen. She refolds the soggy towel around the diminishing ice. "Mac and I went with Livia and another poet to a café. We drank tea and listened and

35

talked and I felt stupid, really stupid. After four years of college."

Sheila's hair is soaked where she's been holding the ice—that energetic hair, looking now as if it's had a long swim of its own and has barely made it back to shore. Kate senses her painting behind her, but her daughter is in front of her. She moves to Sheila, lifts the ice pack to touch the bruise. It doesn't hurt as much when Kate touches it as when Sheila touches it herself.

"I think it will be all right," Sheila says.

Kate asks, "Shall I run down and get you more ice?"

"No. Wait a minute. I've got more to say. About Mac. You won't believe—I mean, we've only seen each other on vacations and stuff for two years. He's been doing Cinderella work for that film company, trying to figure out how to get to be a cinematographer or whatever it is he'll finally do. I've been thinking of him as—oh, a terrific friend. He's helpful, looks out for people. He's sensible. He takes his photography seriously."

"He's nice. Genuinely nice."

"He wants us to get married." Sheila leans over in the chair and sobs.

Kate can't help. Sheila can't stay asleep and innocent like Chagall's woman in the tree. Kate imagines that woman falling from her lush pink nest, rushing downward through leaves and branches and the impersonal air, falling, trying to grasp at something familiar. Kate feels herself fall, too. She takes a long, steadying breath. It's an ordinary morning. Just Saturday. Saturday, July 12. Wait. It's Audrey's birthday. That's why she called. And where's Alex? He's been working a lot at the committee, but not on Saturdays.

Sheila still has her head down. "I don't know where I want to be this summer," she mumbles.

"Let's talk in the car."

"What car?"

"Mine. Audrey's coming at four. It's her birthday. I forgot. We're going to have to go out and buy her a present and get wonderful food for dinner. What time is it?"

Sheila stops sobbing. Bent over, soaked with melted ice and tears, she feels her body slipping away from her. She doesn't have a real body this summer. She panics, jumps out of the chair to be sure she can move. "It's about ten, I guess," she answers, shakily.

"You know what? I just did a little subtracting. It's Audrey's sixty-fifth birthday," Kate says as they move out of the attic to get cleaned up.

Mac bounds onto the porch as Sheila and Kate are leaving the house. Over six feet tall, at least two hundred and ten pounds, Mac played guard on his high school football team. He catches sight of Sheila's bruised forehead, grabs her in his big arms. "You're hurt! It wasn't that bad last night!" He hugs her so the bruise will disappear, thinking he can stop anything threatening with his weight.

"It's not as bad as it looks." Sheila frees herself.

"Listen," Kate says, "we've got to go. Audrey's coming over. It's her birthday. Can you come back around four?"

Mac sees Kate for the first time, blinks at her. As Sheila and Kate hurry across the porch and down the steps, Sheila calls to him, "Come back at four!"

"Hey!" he shouts. He still feels her hair brushing the curly, reddish hair on his arms. He sees Sheila's hair

37

disappear into the car, getting away from him. He heads for Kate's car. "Hey! Can I come with you?"

Sheila rolls down her window while Kate starts the yellow V.W. bug. "Kate and I have shopping to do. Just come back at four. Oh, you know what? You could bring your camera and take some exciting family photos for us."

Kate drives down the hill to Sunset Boulevard and turns left toward Echo Park. Sheila says, "Let's stop at the Avocado. Maybe we can put together a bunch of things for Audrey—lotions and soaps. She loves all that."

In the Avocado, walls are lined with fans that give off faint sandalwood perfume. Balinese masks hang among the fans. There are shelves and shelves of oils for massages, for baths, for feet and hair and hands and eyelids. Kate smells almond oil, especially pungent today. Other odors come at her: tiger lily, black narcissus, fresh lime, China musk, frangipani—sensual and cloying.

There's a new rack of handmade kimonos in the back of the shop. Kate heads for them to escape the insistent luxury of the oils. The kimonos are lovely. Full graceful sleeves. Hand-finished seams. She admires the fabrics— white cranes on a salmon background; red embroidered poppies on black. "That one," Sheila says, nodding at the one Kate's just turned to, a creamy geometric design against burgundy silk. "Audrey would fall on the floor in ecstasy."

Kate checks the price. "It's eighty-five dollars!"

The young woman behind the counter looks like a ripe peach, luscious. Kate fingers the burgundy silk while Sheila and the young woman chat about the shop. The jojoba bean soap. The aloe vera lotion. The specially mixed hair conditioner and the clove toothpaste. Such abundance.

Kate wonders where else this collection of odd riches might exist. Perhaps nowhere quite like this. She loves Los Angeles for its generous, seductive nature and distrusts it for the same things. She's been quiet about her art all these years, hasn't tried to break into the big gallery scene, meet people who could make her famous. There's been Bob. The two one-woman shows he arranged for her were about as much recognition as she can handle. "Deliver me from the artist as movie star," she thinks, but likes the feel of the expensive, silky kimono—red wine, aged to perfection. "We'll take it," she says to the peach.

In the car, Sheila holds the gift-wrapped box on her lap, a white one printed with delicate avocados and circled with satin ribbon. She leans out the window to let the breeze catch her hair. "I'm sorry about yesterday," she says, her words half out of the window, half in the car.

"What is she sorry about?" Kate wonders. "I'm the one who can't stand to see things die, to end." It startles Kate, this being sorry. When Alex stopped painting, when he told Kate he knew she was the artist and he wasn't, he never actually said, "I'm sorry." What he said was, "If I go on painting, I'll have to leap over the edge of a cliff. I see the cliff. I imagine the leap. At the bottom, there's real art in me, but I'd have to leave you to bring it to the surface. I'd have to travel or live alone. Maybe I'd have to go crazy. It scares me. You manage both worlds— this one and the one at the bottom of the cliff. You've made the leap. I can't." Alex opted for his version of reality.

They're into Echo Park now. Kate sees a billboard: "*Descubre Lite—Lite de Miller*" with its broadly smiling

Latino face and a picture of a six pack of Miller Lite beer next to the face. "Sorry?" she says to Sheila.

These days Alex is sitting on a committee that's making decisions about art textbooks for the L.A. City College system. He's a consultant, which means a few months of good money. He wrangled and got almost twice as much as the school system pays consultants, which is some recognition of his knowledge of art in Los Angeles. He's spent years gathering it. If he doesn't paint, he certainly knows painters. Bengston and Francis and Kienholz, and others who aren't so familiar, like Elrod with his minimalist gray pieces, Lois Jarrell with her sprayed acrylic lacquer fairy tales. Alex has a filing cabinet stuffed with slides and notes. "Lord, it's hot," she says. Sheila still has her head out of the window, being sorry.

"Mac. Writing. I don't want to make a big mistake," Sheila says to the street.

"You'll make plenty of big mistakes." Alex saying, "I'm not Picasso," although his early paintings showed real promise. His multitude of jobs, never really in art, never really out of it. Kate slams on the brakes to avoid a cane-waving old man who's marched into the street. "I sold a painting," Kate tells Sheila. "Nine hundred dollars. Don't ask me how Bob Hunt got that much for it, but he did. One of the white ones. There's plenty of money if you want a place of your own for the summer. You're too young to play it safe. Trust yourself." She attacks the accelerator, and the car leaps into a left turn, then a right one into the parking lot of the Trails market.

"Thanks. I don't know. That's a lot of money." Sheila gets out of the car while Kate forms a quick plan for dinner. Mexican food—green enchiladas and beans and rice. A salad. Fresh fruit. The paper banners hanging on the outside wall of the market advertise the day's specials: "Firm, ripe tomatoes—49¢ a pound"; "Cantaloupe—20¢ a pound—serve it with ice cream!" Kate enjoys the wide, colorful lettering. She's been buying food at this store for years. The moose heads over the meat counter vanished ten years ago and were replaced by a large mural of vegetables on the Echo Park Avenue wall of the market, a response to the sensitivities of pro-environment students and artists who came to Echo Park looking for reasonable rents and brown rice.

The aisles are narrow, and there's no way to avoid other shoppers: Latinos with eyes like the Mexican chocolate they buy; elderly people on Social Security who pick out, one by one, six eggs. Blacks, Thais, Vietnamese, Japanese, Koreans. People like Sheila and Kate and Alex who come because the food is inexpensive and fresh and the ambiance isn't too polite. Although the moose heads are gone, there are still three pairs of worn antlers, and, yes, the stuffed owl watches over the ham and bacon case.

Kate locks her car door just as Sheila has done. They've gotten used to locking doors. They even installed a locked gate in the fence around their backyard after a gang of kids—they guess they were kids—had a party in the yard one night when Kate and Alex were away for the weekend and Sheila was at school. There were broken bottles. The lemons had been picked and smashed against the garage and the greenhouse.

Two young Latinos are walking away from the take-out stand at the end of the Trails' parking lot. They move past

41

the red, white, and blue take-out signs advertising Shrimp 'n Chips, Chicken Livers, Chili Dogs, Pizza Burgers, Taquitos, Chicken—toward Kate and Sheila. Carrying cardboard boxes of two or three pieces of fried chicken, they're eating as they walk. White T-shirts. Muscular arms. One of them wears an L.A. Dodgers baseball cap with the visor turned up. Kate notices his sharp, quick face. The other young man—God, it's Ralph, who sees Kate and Sheila and drops a half-eaten chicken breast back in the box, embarrassed. He looks four years older, as he should, than when he and Sheila were dating. He's grown a mustache. Have his eyebrows thickened since high school orchestra? Sheila was the pianist. Ralph was the best trumpet player the school had ever had. He could play baroque fanfares, Handel's Suite in D, Miles Davis's solos, Chuck Mangione's hits. Ralph could play anything, except, finally, Sheila.

"How's it going?" Sheila asks.

"It's going." He gestures with the box of chicken toward his friend. "You remember Danny Lopez?"

Sheila nods. Kate says hello. Ralph and Danny shift awkwardly. Nobody wants to do this. "Still playing?" Sheila asks.

"Yeah," Ralph says. "I'm trying to get through the City College music program. My folks think I should work. Music isn't work to them." Maybe it's that his eyes are shadowy, maybe it isn't the eyebrows at all. "So I take time off from classes to help out in my brother's auto shop. But I'm hanging in there. Danny and I keep the group together. We're picking up gigs. Danny's still the hottest drummer in town, and—" Ralph realizes he's talking too much and lowers his head to check out the hot asphalt of the parking lot.

"How's your family?" Sheila persists.

"Okay. Mostly okay. Gloria's got two kids now." Nods. Smiles. Ralph looks up again. "I'm the only one left at home. Chuy's in the army. Louie's got the auto shop. He's doing good. He says when he makes just a little more bread, he'll marry Linda. Jeez, they've been going together for ten years." Laughs, but tension under the laughter. Four years ago, Sheila went off to college, and Ralph was furious with her, with Kate, with Alex, with Echo Park and Silverlake.

"Your chicken will get cold," Kate says. They're all released.

"I miss him," Sheila says as she and Kate go into the market. "I miss him a lot."

"Why did you break up with him?"

"He scared me."

Ralph would bring his horn to their house on afternoons after school. He'd sit on the porch playing the blues or old standards like "My Funny Valentine" for Sheila. The horn would play through the house and through Kate, too, as she listened. She was always listening—and looking. Ralph with those firm arms, that skin of his. His Indian and Spanish ancestors gave Ralph skin the brown of mysterious liquor, exciting and filling.

He stayed for dinner and said thank you every time they passed him the butter or looked as if they might pass it. He said thank you for letting me stay, thank you for letting me be with Sheila, thank you for talking to me and offering me a beer, which nobody at my house will do yet, since

I'm the youngest, and the youngest is a prince but not a man at my house. Thank you for not being my family, for having time for art and letting me see that some people live like this.

They weren't his family. Finally, they weren't even his friends. Sheila decided that she had to go to college in San Francisco to move toward herself and her writing, to get into her own life. Ralph had never stopped playing his trumpet long enough to let her hear anything else.

"I'm sorry," Kate said to him the night that Sheila couldn't say it. It was a few days before Sheila was to leave for college. Ralph was trying to make plans to see her on weekends. Kate could hear them out on the porch, arguing and kissing and arguing. Then Sheila came into the house. Kate saw her from the kitchen where she and Alex were drinking coffee. Sheila rushed upstairs. Ralph stayed on the porch, listening, himself, for once—listening for her to come back, listening for anything but this to happen.

"Want some coffee?" Kate had called to him.

He sat with them for a couple of minutes, eerily still, every muscle shivering. Then he got up, knocked over his chair, jumped back—surprised that he'd overturned the chair. He picked it up and said, "I'll never see you again." He fled. Kate followed him out of the house and said, as he turned and glared at her as if he might knock her over as he had the chair, "I'm sorry."

Inside the noisy store, Kate pulls a shopping cart from the row of carts, thinking, "It doesn't make any difference that I apologized to Ralph for Sheila, or that Alex keeps apologizing for giving up painting by taking jobs so I can paint. Or that Sheila tells me she's sorry for yesterday. We are sorry for how things are. We want to extinguish pain, which is impossible." During the time she thought of killing herself, in the days of white paint and Sheila's menstrual blood and the spider tattooed on everything, one voice in her said, every time she wanted to turn on the gas, "How dare you?"

They drink another toast—this one to 1947, to Audrey's arrival in Los Angeles. "It was the *perfect* time to come here," Audrey says. "California sportswear was just about to sweep the country." They drink a toast to sportswear, to those shorts, slacks, bathing suits that swept eastward from Los Angeles to New York, Chicago, to places that were ready for what later became known as "casual wear." Then they drink a toast to Audrey's career—to her thirty-three years at West Coast Sportswear; to her job as typist, as secretary, as assistant to the assistant vice-president. A toast to her knocking off the word "assistant" every time she moved up. A toast to her vice-presidency in charge of sales. "This year," Audrey pronounces, "your best bet is beige, nothing but timeless beige, blushing from a little shocking lavender."

The living room has relaxed into the kind of comfortable disarray that will be a horror tomorrow. Glasses, sticky dessert plates, the gift box with yards of tissue paper trailing on the floor, a few decorative candles melting onto the old wooden chest in the corner, photo albums from the very top of the closet—Audrey asked Kate to drag those out and pass them around for everyone to say how much or how little Audrey has changed. There's a beach shot:

Flo and Audrey and Kate leaning on Flo's Chevy, grinning, hoping that California would smile, too. Divorce. Death. Loneliness. The Three Agonies, trying to start over. Their bathing suits are the West Coast Sportswear suit of the year: a two-piece, shirred number that makes them look like babies in sunsuits.

The champagne has held center stage since dinner. So has Audrey. Her 1940s perkiness has mellowed into something she'd call verve; something Kate would call overbearing self-assurance. Mac, an unobtrusive photographer in spite of his size, has moved quietly from spot to spot around the room. His 1971, 35-mm Nikon hangs around his neck, ready. He angles himself into the corner behind the piano to get a shot of Audrey proclaiming herself vice-president in charge of birthdays.

Alex has spent the evening refilling everyone's champagne glass and telling stories about his committee. "Could he have been working today?" Kate asks herself. He got home about five, rolled cheese and chilies into corn tortillas to make the most lavish enchiladas ever produced in the family, covered with spicy salsa, frosted with sour cream, topped with black olives. Then he dashed out for the champagne. "As if it's *his* birthday," Kate thinks. She rocks in the chair she's retrieved from the porch, watches her family, smells the star jasmine through the open front door. Audrey did almost fall to the floor in ecstasy, as Sheila predicted. She has the kimono on over her tailored pantsuit. Its sleeves, like wings, italicize everything she says. "I'm positive that the electric streetcars absolutely *disappeared* no later than 1958." Audrey lifts her champagne glass to Alex, and the burgundy silk sleeve sails toward him, too, as if it's sweeping the country like her sportswear.

"Come on, I know some L.A. history," Alex tells her. "The streetcars were taken out in '60."

It was 1961, but Kate avoids such moments between Alex and Audrey, their arguments about dates, facts, addresses, titles of books. They embroil themselves in these things just to keep the friction of the past alive, though neither of them really cares about the streetcars' demise.

Audrey stopped her real fighting with Alex when he and Kate bought this house. Before that, for the first years they were married, Kate did her best to enliven the cheap apartments they rented with what was known as "Ginkle Modern," after a discount store called Ginkle's. Artists on tight budgets bought Ginkle chairs—metal frames that looked like two crossed propellers. A couple of those with bright covers stretched over them, pillows on the floor— a room was furnished. Audrey hated struggling in and out of the chairs; she hated the inexpensive dinners of lentil stew. Alex had led Kate into this life. Audrey hated him for that and for being Jewish.

She never said it. She'd accuse Alex of encouraging Kate to be an artist. That was fair game. She'd mutter about his not doing things "our way," but she'd been influenced enough by Flo to hesitate about judging people by the accident of birth. Still, she couldn't help herself. She didn't want her daughter's last name to be Levinsky or her granddaughter to be half-Jewish. Audrey realized she was wrong. She'd been on the receiving end of plenty of prejudice when she was moving up in the company. "You want a woman for that job? She'll be a nervous

47

wreck or pregnant in six months." Audrey knew it well, the hot fury in her because she couldn't do anything about her sex. Alex can't do anything about his religion. It makes her mad. There's so much nobody can do anything about. She consoles herself with Alex's grandfather. A rabbi in the family. She glances at him next to her on the couch. Is he starting to look like a rabbi? After all, he's forty-five. It's time he started to look like something.

Kate never met Grandfather Levinsky, although she hears his ghost with them in the house, humming, giving soft advice. Alex repeats his sayings: "Have pity on lofty matters." "Safety is not goodness." The old man, a widower, lived with Alex's family while Alex was growing up. Grandfather Levinsky helped Alex see the imbalance between Sol and Alex's mother and sisters. Kate is sure he's still helping them. She rocks as Audrey flaps around the room, posing for Mac.

When they bought this house, Audrey surprised them by throwing a housewarming. They'd moved a few things in but were sleeping in the last cheap apartment. When they arrived one Sunday morning with Sheila, age seven, and a load of books, they found twenty of their friends waiting with breakfast. Their friends. Audrey had surrendered as much as she could.

Kate surveys the room. Everyone except Audrey is wearing jeans. One of Audrey's crusades has been to eliminate jeans from the world. Levi Strauss himself could go hang. They're all wearing T-shirts, too. Alex has said that the cultural legacy of the '70s has been T-shirts that talk. Kate's says, "Most Valuable Player," a joke from Alex. Mac's wearing one he's had for a long time, completely stretched out of shape, but the rubbery outlines of the word "Casablanca" and of the familiar heads of Ingrid Bergman and Humphrey Bogart are clear. Mac's a *Casablanca* fan. Valiant souls, he believes, under pressure of war and love and conflict, will do the right thing. The movie has become his amulet against dismay, his hope that his present thankless job at the film company will turn into a chance to show how valiant he can be, how decisive, how effective with his camera. His camera always tells the truth.

Mac stands next to Sheila. She's sitting at the baby grand, slightly behind everybody. He slips his camera to his eye, breathes in, and, sure enough, Alex and Audrey's argument over the best place in Los Angeles to buy doughnuts is immortalized.

Sheila plays "Happy Birthday" with every toast, then lapses into furry little melodies, snatches of things she used to play. "My Funny Valentine" gives Kate a start. "Sheila misses Ralph, but he scared her. Mac wants to marry her, which makes her afraid of making mistakes. A young woman loses her virginity in so many ways. She gives her body to boys, to menstruating, to crying, to school, then retreats and says, 'What am I going to do?' Then she gives again, retreats again." Sheila's T-shirt is a souvenir of a women's writing conference at San Francisco State. On the front is a typewriter with a bunch of flowers growing out of its bed of keys. There hasn't been time for her to write today, has there? And now she plays these old songs to herself.

The star jasmine teases Kate's nostrils. So does the champagne. She's not drunk, but she's not sober. Her mother's sleeves fly in her nose as Audrey flaps back to the couch to settle next to Alex again. Grandfather Levinsky squeezes between them, stretching his arms across the couch, embracing their banter. He smiles at Kate, a smile that matches her sense of the evening—memory, tension, pleasure, the mess of life, the ever-changing–never-ending mess of love. Sheila plays "Happy Birthday" one last time. They're toasting her bruise, which has become a source of mock worry and bad jokes as the evening's grown woozy. Kate doesn't raise her glass. She thinks she hears something on the porch. No, nothing. Just Grandfather Levinsky, leaving.

"I'll get more champagne," Alex says, heading for the kitchen, Groucho Marx leering from his T-shirt.

"Mac and I are going over to his place." Sheila's behind Kate, whispering in her ear. "We'll slip out the back. Mac's car is parked out there. I'm going to give Audrey a quick goodbye and say good night to Dad on our way through the kitchen." Kate wants Sheila here, close to her, but says, "Good night, dear one. Good night, Mac. Thanks for taking pictures."

Alex returns with a fresh bottle of hissing champagne, but Audrey's dozing on the couch, clutching her empty glass. Alex puts the bottle in Kate's lap, hugs her, says, "You wanna take this baby upstairs and finish off the evening?" She does.

"Let me get Audrey to bed in the study. I don't want her driving tonight." Kate gets up, not as unsteady as she'd expected. "Where were you today?"

"With Sam Nakamura," he says, and heads for the stairs. Sam. Kate hasn't heard anything about him for a long time.

50

Audrey's willing to stay, delighted to let Kate hang the kimono right next to the bed on a chair so it will be the first thing she sees in the morning. "Happy Birthday," Kate says as she closes the door to the study behind her. She'll try to take a solitary walk tomorrow before anybody else gets up. She goes to the front door to close and lock it. These California nights that cool off after the heat of the day are the best part of summer. She steps outside to breathe a little more jasmine. Almost beyond the reach of the porch light, she can decipher a shape, and, as she keeps looking, it comes clearer. Ralph is on the bottom step of the porch with his trumpet case next to him and a brown paper bag on top of the case. Kate knows what's in the bag—a can of the hottest chilies in the world, stuffed with tuna, from the Trails. Sheila and Ralph used to sit out here and eat those things, laughing with burned tongues, teasing. Who could eat the most, the fastest? When Sheila won, Ralph would say, "You'll make a great Chicana." He's hunched over, his forearms resting on his thighs. His head is down, invisible to Kate. He doesn't move. He doesn't look as if he's going to move, either.

Audrey's head swims. The house has been dark for half an hour, but she can't sleep. She won't sleep. She shoves the sheet off her legs and struggles to sit up, determined to get a handle on things before she tells Kate in the morning about retiring.

What a week. Cleaning out years of stuff, putting up with her secretary's insufferable weeping every time Audrey had her haul another box of outdated files to the trash. "We won't know what to do without you," Midge had whined at every opportunity.

"Just ask me," was what Audrey had said to prove her competence at West Coast Sportswear, until she'd hit the top and everybody did ask her. Her sales staff respected her tough-minded fairness. The designers consulted her on fabrics and colors, which weren't even her realm. All the secretaries came to her when they couldn't get along with their bosses. "Rock of Gibraltar to the end," she thinks, proud of fending off three invitations to farewell lunches. "Who wants to watch them all crying into the salmon mousse? One nice party was enough."

She slips awkwardly out of bed, wearing only panties. "Drink a lot of water," she thinks, making her way to the kitchen in the dark, feeling along the walls. "Don't throw up," she warns herself as she downs two glasses of water at the sink. She wavers back to the living room and lies on the couch. Her head pounds less insistently. Now she can decide what to do with the rest of her life.

Scenes from the week intrude. Midge and her cohorts bringing a bouquet of lavender roses, Audrey's favorite flower, to the retirement party. Allan McNamara's speech— he praised Audrey's "impeccable business instincts." They gave her a gold bracelet, a plain circle but the real thing, with "Best Wishes" engraved inside.

She tries to focus on the future. She won't have to get up at 6 A.M. or work on Saturdays if they need her. She won't have to catch herself before she screams, "That's disgusting!" about some bizarre new fashion trend. She can be herself. The Rock. No, that's over. She can be— she slips toward sleep, then jerks herself awake, stares into the dark as Kate did last night, wondering what pattern is being made on the shadowed ceiling.

"Why did you have to die, Roy?" she thinks, startled; she doesn't allow memories of her husband. But a rush of sweet air brushes her face like one of his kisses. "He took such good care of me, rubbed my back after those ten-hour days at the drugstore. Said we'd get rich, move to Detroit or Chicago, have more babies." She could plan her future then: She and Roy would grow old together. He'd kissed her. He'd promised.

"My hair will be a mess." She sits up abruptly. "I should drive home so nobody will have to look at me in the morning." But sitting up makes her head reel. Well, they can't find her on the couch in only her panties. She eases back to the study, fingers the silk of her kimono. "Sheila picked it out. She'd look terrific in one herself. That handsome boyfriend of hers—Mac? Zach?—adores her whatever she wears, I guess. I might be a great-grandmother soon." Audrey imagines holding a tiny baby, goo-gooing at it. It would be nice to sleep in the kimono, but it would wrinkle. The silk feels—

She stops herself. Roy's mouth. Not now.

"All our luck and love to you for your new adventures," Midge had written on the card attached to the roses. Audrey has to make some decisions. Get those new adventures going. She reaches for her pantsuit, thinking she'll go home, whatever condition her head is in, but she stumbles and barely catches herself before she falls. For now, sinking back into bed is all the adventure she can manage.

3

THE HOT, DRY SKY has relented. An overcast morning gray cools and reassures Kate as she drives north
along Vermont Avenue toward Griffith Park and its miles
of hiking trails. She passes Rocco's, the Italian restaurant
where hopeful opera singers accompany the lasagna, and
the Middle Eastern grocery with its pyramids of cheese
and pastries in the window. There's W.C.W.'s, the bookstore; the tiny Japanese restaurant tucked between
W.C.W.'s and the movie theater; the post office on the
other side of the street next to the pie shop.

A little farther on, she passes rows of apartment buildings—familiar Los Angeles versions of ten or twelve units
facing a swimming pool, the major attraction of these places,
though Kate rarely sees anyone swimming in them. The
pools are too small for real swimming, but the water, clean
and blue and chlorinated, waits for someone: for a woman

who has rented one of these apartments just so she can step right out of her living room and onto the patio and into the water on a morning like this. No one will be watching so early on Sunday; no one will notice if she's a little overweight or repeatedly tests the water with her foot. An older woman. She lives alone and likes the neighborhood because she can walk to the pie shop and get a bowl of soup and a piece of banana cream pie, then to the movies if the theater isn't playing anything too foreign or obscure.

Kate notices these apartment women—widowed or divorced or otherwise alone—in this area so often that she really believes, as she drives past the Griffith Arms and the Los Feliz Lanai, that a woman is pulling on her bathing suit and will soon come out for a swim before breakfast.

Beyond the apartments, beyond Los Feliz Boulevard, the street is lined with grand trees, their trunks as heavy and wrinkled as elephant hide, proof of age. Some things last in this city of change. The houses become large, stately— brick monuments. Kate slows down as she moves into the park, then stops across from the Greek Theatre where her favorite trail heads up, into the hills.

She's hiked this trail many times but is always surprised by the quick shifts of sunlight and shade, by the abundance of foliage so close to the city. Silent, welcoming. Pink oleander blooms hang gently on their bushes. Wild tobacco nods. Its yellow flowers, as thin as children's fingers, dangle over the trail. No one is here this morning except Kate, yet the dusty trail is a map of footprints—waffle-bottomed walking shoes next to zigzag soles on top of the patterned geometry of scores of tennis shoes.

At the first rise of the trail, she's breathing hard enough to notice that she's breathing. The high rises of downtown crowd her view. Los Angeles builds rather than restores. Tear down the old houses, churches, theaters, and you won't be reminded that you'll soon be old, too. Demolish historic craftsmanship and build a twelve unit apartment where a woman wants to swim in a pool that isn't large enough to swim in, and she may not get in the water at all if she looks in the mirror and decides that she's, well, really too heavy to be seen in her bathing suit, even if there's no one to see her. Her thighs fold at the edge of the suit. Last night on TV, she noticed that the older women stood behind counters selling paper towels while the younger ones were lying on beds selling perfume. Aging. Audrey was sixty-five yesterday. "This trail," Kate thinks, "how old is it?" She knows there are shale and limestone deposits nearby from the Miocene, and north of here there's the site of a Spanish limekiln.

Our Lady of the Queen of the Angels. On August 2, 1769, Portolá came upon a river and an Indian village and a wide, arable plain. He named the river *Río de Nuestra Señora la Reina de Los Angeles de Porciúncula,* and two years later a town was born. Kate stands, gazing at its multi-storied buildings, the vast grid of streets. Twenty-four-hour markets and pharmacies and movie houses and restaurants. The older woman can eat her piece of pie at 3 P.M. or 3 A.M. Under the pie shop, the land was first Indian, then Spanish, then everything at once. Around-the-clock land.

The trail is eroded from last winter's rains. Kate watches where she sets her feet, stepping through the gullies and humps in the ground. Hard beans, like jewels, drop from small plants, their shells circled with black and gray. Their definite, intricate patterns remind her of Sam Nakamura—tough, lucid, complex. Alex was with him yesterday. It's been a couple of years since Kate's seen him, although he lives a short distance from them, burrowed into a Silverlake hill.

Sam taught painting at Gill Institute while Kate and Alex were students. "He must be Audrey's age," Kate muses. Japanese-American, he never forgave America for the humiliation of Manzanar, a relocation camp in World War II. He was American and always had been. He was forced away from his art while Kate and her playmates were chanting at elementary school recess, "Do you like cheese? Dirty Japanese!" After Manzanar, Sam relinquished Japanese formality. He became bitter and direct. If life was harsh, Sam would match it. Gill reserved him for advanced students. By the time Alex and Kate were ready for his classes, they'd heard enough about him to want to make friends. They weren't great sufferers, as passionate and unrelenting as the kind of people Sam admired, but neither were they afraid to be tested, they told themselves.

They'd been slowly learning each other since the eggplant painting. For a while, they pretended it was an intellectual relationship, an intense meeting of minds, an ongoing debate about Abstract Expressionism. But Kate and Alex couldn't be only painters with each other for long. He had immediately fallen in love with her precision and imagination but also with her cheekbones, her ankles, her throaty voice. She was excited by his ideas, his spirit, and couldn't

57

resist reaching across the cafeteria table, where they primed themselves for Sam's classes with coffee and doughnuts, to ruffle his thick hair. They ended up making love in Alex's warehouse loft when his three roommates were out. In that loft they began, at least, to understand passion.

No line could exist on a canvas without Sam's asking, "Where did that line come from? Why does it exist in the world? There aren't any rules in art except the perfect gesture, the absolute line. This line is not inevitable. It could have been a goddamn circle. This line stinks." Kate sinks into a tiny valley of pines where the air is cold and damp. It isn't summer here, but autumn. She steps into the fresh chill. Summer doesn't last long. When Kate sees Sheila, she sees herself at the time when she and Alex were studying with Sam. She remembers how her breasts would swell—visibly, she thought—when she'd run into Alex in a hallway or at a sink where they'd be cleaning brushes. She doesn't have those breasts anymore. Sheila has them. Kate wears Alex's shirts and loose T-shirts and blouses that hang over pants. Her breasts aren't wonderful now. She plants her feet on the upward trail. Sun pushes among the roots that coil out of the side of the hill. She doesn't want Sheila's breasts. Yet as she glances under the open neck of her shirt, she sees the imbalance—one breast a little lower than the other when she doesn't wear a bra, and she rarely wears a bra. Her nipples are just nipples, not Persian fantasies outlined in rouge. Her body feels so much like what it is: a dependable body, not a constant surprise. Sensuality doesn't fade, but that fiery excitement does. Kate sees Sheila and remembers having a body that could be shocked and aroused and released by Alex, by nothing but touching his hair, by not even touching—by the sight of a painting that captured all Sam was teaching them—or by the vision of a glazed doughnut on a white plate next to a coffee cup. Here was Alex, this dark Jewish man. Here was a way to be an artist; here was a way to worship.

She hits the top of the trail, gulping for breath. She turns to look back at what she's just walked and glimpses the great domes of the observatory in the distance. She breaks into the old hymn from her childhood, ". . . came a vision of Holy Grail / and a voice in the waiting night / Follow, follow, follow the gleam. . . ." She can't sing it as stoutly as she'd like since she's out of breath, but she sings, anyway, until an old man, lean and tanned, in boots and walking shorts, comes up the trail. His two eager dogs find her and sniff at her feet. He calls to them, says, "Good morning!" as he passes her. His legs are healthy, but skinny rather than lean. He's frailer than he seems. Audrey. Is she all right? She looked defenseless last night, her face loosened by champagne. She's probably still asleep or just barely up, but Kate's suddenly worried. This summer. Everything abundant. Everything dying. She moves down the trail as fast as she can.

"This kitchen could use a coat of paint," Audrey's saying as Kate comes in the back door. "I thought you people were doing okay, moneywise."

"We're okay," Alex says, setting a coffee mug on the table for Kate. She sits with them, untying and pulling off her tennis shoes and socks as Alex pours coffee. Audrey frowns at the yellow kitchen walls, faded by light and use.

59

Her well-set hair—still blond, with help, highlighted by silver streaks—survived the night. Her white pantsuit is only slightly crumpled from a night of hanging over a chair. She stops looking at the walls and looks at something else, invisible, far away. Kate waits, "the way I used to wait for her to come home when I was a kid and we lived in that pink stucco place. Dreading her arrival and hoping for it at any minute. She criticized me so much—the best daughter was supposed to do everything right." Audrey didn't have time for a child, only for someone who could talk intelligently, understand things quickly, who could be, Kate guessed, a good employee. Yet Kate yearned for their meals together, for the time they shared.

Audrey can't get her hand into her pants pocket as she sits, so she finally stands up and pulls out a linen hand-kerchief. "Yesterday," she announces, "was my last day at work. I retired." She can't resist a few tears but says sternly, "It's nothing to cry about."

Kate lifts her mug in a toast, but Audrey doesn't reach for hers. She stands folding and unfolding the handker-chief, getting ready, Kate suspects, to make a speech.

"You didn't guess, did you?" Audrey asks. Kate shakes her head. "Thirty-three years. You thought I'd go on forever, didn't you?" Kate shrugs. She's thought of Audrey's age but not her retirement. "Thirty-three years of complete devotion to good products, marketed with taste. I could sell the most ordinary cotton casual dress if it was well made. Good products mean good sales, and, believe me, I was the best vice-president in charge of sales West Coast ever had. They knew it, too. They begged me to stay. You didn't know your mother was being begged to stay, did you?" Kate mouths a "no." "But for—oh, six months or so—I was getting tired right after lunch. How many catnaps can you take in the ladies' room before somebody notices? My ulcer doesn't flare up very often, but when it does—how much Mylanta can you gulp down on a break before somebody teases you about your white mustache? I didn't want to stay if I couldn't do the job I'd always done. And I sure didn't want to collapse and be dragged out mumbling about getting the 1947 line into the stores." She leans across the table, her face close to Kate's. "You know, when I'd see one of West Coast's pieces on the street—a terrific jumpsuit or pair of pants— I'd say to myself, 'There's a great item of clothing that isn't going to waste.' I'd be tempted to go over to that person and say, 'You wouldn't be wearing that stunning outfit if it weren't for me.' It's good to know I haven't wasted my life." She sits down heavily.

"Did they do something for you when you left? Give you a party, at least?"

"A little get-together."

"You didn't tell us?"

"I didn't think of it."

"This was your retirement party and you didn't think of asking us?"

"I didn't think you'd want to come."

"We would have come!"

"I know my job has always been too capitalistic for you and Alex—your artists' souls. I didn't want any lifted eyebrows from you about my job."

"We wouldn't have lifted any eyebrows." Kate could use help with Audrey, but Alex only stares into his coffee.

61

He hasn't said anything about why he went to see Sam yesterday, after so long. Alex hasn't said much of anything for weeks.

"I didn't think you'd even remember my birthday," Audrey says. "I had to get on the phone and call you to even see you."

"But we did celebrate, didn't we?"

"I haven't wasted my life, have I?" Audrey presses her handkerchief to her mouth as if she can put these words back into herself before anyone knows she's said them.

Audrey doesn't cry, ever. Kate watches her try to hold back her tears and says quietly, "We love you. We may not all have the same kinds of lives, but we certainly love you and respect your work."

Alex interrupts, "How are you set financially?"

The worst possible question. Kate's sure Audrey will spit out that she'll go to a rest home and they can forget about her the way everybody forgets mothers and fathers these days. Instead, Audrey brightens, glad to talk over practical matters. She and Alex chat about her retirement benefits and insurance policies.

The plants on the windowsill—parsley and thyme and basil—overflow toward the sink. Kate gets up to pick off the too-long shoots while Alex and Audrey talk. She stands barefoot at the sink, hurt by her mother, as always; loving her mother. As always.

She begins to do the dishes from last night, thinking, "Audrey's going to be lonely. She'll sit in her lovely house that's so beautifully decorated it couldn't take one more 'touch' of anything, and she's going to have to think about herself, about those quick terrors in the middle of the night when she wakes up and knows that she's really going to die." Kate pauses over a champagne glass. It was a good party. They should have danced, though. She'd like to dance right now. She'd like to pull Audrey off her feet, out of her pantsuit, into the autumnal hollow in the park. They'd throw herbs all over themselves like sinless old pagans and dance their lopsided breasts, their lined faces, their fear of wasted lives, straight into heaven.

Sheila wakes up at Mac's as Kate heads for Griffith Park. She's comfortable, happy to be in bed with Mac, thinking that marrying him might not be a bad idea. He's gentle and sensible and, well, really good for her. He had answers last night: forget about renting her own place, marry him in September, and if she wants to continue school, find a graduate writing program nearby, maybe at U.C. Irvine. She could probably get a scholarship or loan so she wouldn't have to work. They couldn't both live on Mac's salary, but he hopes his company will promote him soon. He's been talking to one of the producers who does documentaries. His next project will need a photographer to travel around the country, filming wild animal life. Mac might, just might, be that guy. That would mean more money, a big step in Mac's career. They can't wait forever, can they? They have to work these things out.

The morning light reaches her, still gray. She's ready to get up but doesn't want to disturb Mac. He breathes evenly, sleeping, beside her. They stayed up so late last night talking. She'll get dressed, make a cup of instant coffee, enjoy watching Mac sleep for a few minutes, then go home to get some writing done.

Yellow daisies push up from the typewriter across her T-shirt, with "Women Growing Their Own Words" above the daisies and "San Francisco State Writing Conference" under the typewriter. She moves easily along the street, covering the mile and a half to her house without effort. Sheila has never faced a bad winter, relentless cold making harsh red marks on the backs of legs where boots constantly rub, weather that can freeze hopes. She walks with her shoulders back, never having had to hunch against piercing wind.

That line of Livia's echoes: "No directions for coming alive, but every shape throws its sparks." She could take off from that, write her own piece—a prose poem, maybe—about coming alive at twenty-two, having a future. She believes, suddenly, in the future, in herself as a fine writer, in Mac. By the time she's at her backyard, she's filled with metaphor, images, theme weaving with theme. She unlocks the gate. It would be nice to sit in one of the lawn chairs for a while. This morning silence, a time to imagine anything she wants to, never lasts long enough. That's why she looks out of her bedroom window the first thing in the morning. Her mind gets free.

But instead of sitting down, she wanders to the end of the yard, to the greenhouse where she played as a child, a good place to be alone. "Sheila." A whisper. Ralph, in the greenhouse, waiting for her, waiting to take her back to four years ago, except that it isn't four years ago. It's Sunday, this Sunday, right now.

She opens the wobbly door slowly. Ralph, a muscular shadow, sits on the earth floor, his legs crossed, unmoving. "I called you and you came," he says. "I've been here all night, making the music to bring you back."

The shape of his horn case is next to him. "Didn't somebody hear your trumpet?"

"I played in my mind. On your porch. Then all over the backyard, then here. My horn, ripe and hungry. Your piano. That sweet touch of yours. Played our music together in my mind and called you back."

She eases to the floor in front of him, smelling the old soil under her. Their knees meet. Gradually, she makes out his face in the dim light. They've never made love, but she knows lovemaking now and knows what she sees in his eyes that are as brown as the earth they sit on.

"It has to be," he says. "I've hung around Echo Park, around and around, knowing you'd come home from school and you'd know, too, that it has to be. You're music, Sheila. I'm music. Why did you leave music to go away? You were scared."

The bag of explosive chilies stuffed with tuna is on top of the trumpet case. High school. She and Ralph, hanging out with Danny and all the musicians in the orchestra at parties. Then she and Ralph would sneak off to his car to kiss, to talk in a rambling language that was another kind of music. She'd never talked with anyone else like that. Ralph's mysterious thinking made her think like him. He had a soul name that a coyote in the mountains had given him once when he'd taken peyote. He wouldn't tell her the name, only that he had it, that she had one, too, and she'd find it if she stayed with him.

Sure, she was scared. Of the intensity, of going into his world and never coming back to her own. They sit now for a long time, knees together, breathing together, and she feels more excitement than she's felt with Mac, more than she felt with her first real lover in San Francisco. "I'm not scared now," she whispers.

Ralph pushes her to the floor of the greenhouse. She moves her hand along the rich skin of his arm and is ready to give in to how much she wanted him four years ago, and she laughs, under him, but the laughing turns to gulping, choking that's foolish and ugly to her. She realizes where she is. In her backyard. In the shack where she used to play Batman and Robin and rescue the victims of the world. She shoves him and says, "Not like this."

He hears her choke, backs off, says, "God, are you okay?" as she jumps up, thinks there's one more minute to lie back down, let him take her, which is what she wants, but isn't, isn't at all what she wants.

He helps her brush off her jeans and T-shirt, still talking about music. She crosses the yard alone and goes into the house where Audrey's mixing batter for crepes. "Nobody's even had breakfast," Audrey thinks. "It'll be brunch, then. Fruit crepes with sour cream. I'll show them. I'm not going to be an old biddy who dies a year after she retires because she can't stand not working. I'll stand it. I'll cook and entertain, take classes, enjoy myself. Isn't that what—what is it they call it on TV ads—the 'second half'—isn't that what the second half is all about?"

Grandmother and granddaughter meet now in the kitchen and hug as they haven't hugged since Audrey got Sheila a bicycle for her eleventh birthday. They meet—both ashamed that they can't control what happens to them— how young or old they are, how foolish, how overwhelmed, how very lonely they are, standing in the kitchen, holding each other.

Kate's in the study. The dishes done—every last sticky

plate from the party—she plops into a chair for a minute before she makes up Audrey's bed. Alex peeks in, his eyebrows pulled together, giving him the owl look—disturbed, though, not wise. "Hi," she says, wondering if he has something to say about Audrey's retirement that he couldn't say in the kitchen, but his face looks cloudier than Audrey could make it. He shuffles through papers on his desk, rubs his hand across his forehead, finally settles on the rumpled bed and says, "This summer I have to do something for myself."

Kate feels the coolness of the bedroom yesterday as he left her, as she thought of how the owls are disappearing from the neighborhood. "What do you have to do?"

He starts to lean back on the bed but stops himself, pulls himself up from the bed to stand by the desk again, the desk he inherited from his grandfather. "I want to learn to paint again. It's not too late. Sam showed me the work he's been doing—action paintings on huge sheets of canvas. He hears the paintings happen, he says. The older he gets, the better he gets. Things speak to him, Kate. I started to hear sounds, too—the way I used to—the vibrations of color. I got high, absolutely high, from spending the day with Sam, away from here."

Kate sits where she is but wishes it were another day in another year.

"Sheila's so damned beautiful," he goes on. "I can't bear to see her. I don't feel like her father but like a useless fool who just hangs around. I can't do a thing for her. You've got your own art. I want mine. I deserve—" He thrusts his hand through his graying, feathery hair. "I've felt so left out."

Mac wakes up, finds the note Sheila left for him signed,

67

"Love, love, love," and is sure they'll get married in September. He maneuvers his darkroom equipment out of the way in the bathroom and takes a long shower, then eats breakfast, picking up his camera in the middle of it to get a shot of the pattern the silverware and plate make against the texture of the table. He remembers the two rolls of film from the party last night and decides to spend time with them after breakfast in his bathroom darkroom.

4

"BUT THERE AREN'T any pictures of you," Kate says to Mac as she studies the proof sheet and eight by tens he's handed her.

"Photographer's hazard." He sits across from her at the round oak table where they've spread out the pictures, grins, and shoves thick, red blond hair off his face with his forearm.

"I like this one of Sheila," Kate says, bending over the proof sheet, tapping with Mac's magnifying glass. Sheila at the piano last night. She looks as if someone's calling her name—surprise and recognition around her mouth. "It's lovely." She pulls the proof sheet closer and squints through the magnifying glass. "You're good at portraits."

Mac shifts, embarrassed, in the wooden chair. The chair squeaks, a familiar creaking like a family pet's meow. Last Christmas, he sat here at the table with Kate, and they talked about photography and painting. She and Alex had invited him to their holiday get-togethers for friends. She'd take a few minutes away from everybody else to replenish the food, and Mac would follow to see if he could help. They'd end up sitting at the table while the Swedish meatballs reheated. He'd ask questions about Kate's conception of light, of foreground and background. They'd talk until they smelled the meatballs burning.

Kate looks up from the proof sheet at Mac, plotting the levels and planes, the shadows and highlights in his face. "Those barely visible lines around his eyes, like scratches—they'll be his old age someday." Mac feels her examining him. The chair meows and teeters. He steadies himself, then reaches across the table for the proof sheet.

"Here's one of you that would be great enlarged." He points to a muddy shot. "It's pretty dark, but I think I can bring it up."

Kate finds herself in the photo, barely herself, in the rocking chair, exchanging looks with Grandfather Levinsky as he sat on the couch.

"It's the only one of you alone, so I'd like to print it. I could do the photo of Sheila and this—mother and daughter."

"Get your camera and I'll take a couple of pictures of you."

"Ah, you don't have to."

"I want to."

"I'm too shy for this stuff."

Kate picks up one of the eight by tens. Alex, lifting his champagne glass. She understands why he was in such a good mood. Sam. The revelation that Alex has to live for himself now. "I've felt so left out," she hears him say, as he said it this morning, as he said it again when he left the study to go over to Sam's for another dose of encouragement.

There had been a lot of champagne at their wedding reception, too. "Hardly a reception, but what fun I had." They all had fun at Rocco's, the Italian restaurant on Vermont, around a table for ten, feasting after Kate and Alex's brief ceremony at the county courthouse at noon. Audrey was Kate's attendant; Sam was Alex's. The others were Alex's three roommates, Flo, and two girlfriends of Kate's from art school, dressed, even for a wedding, in black leotards and black skirts.

Kate wouldn't wear white, though Audrey insisted that white for a first wedding was the only proper thing. Kate wanted a bright color, a dress nobody would mistake for a work dress or even a party dress. She didn't want white lace and gobs of net. She would have worn outlandish gold lamé—ah, gold lamé and ostrich feathers. She mentioned this to Audrey, who was fairly sure Kate was kidding, but Kate wasn't laughing when she said it. Playing on Audrey's horror, she went even further. "I know a feather supply house in the garment district—Vrotell's—you've heard of it. Maybe we'll go down there tomorrow and see what we can find." Then she couldn't keep up the joke, felt her mouth give, shake, then really laugh. She and Audrey fell on Audrey's living room couch, laughing over how many feathers it would take to cover Kate's body completely.

Audrey didn't want Kate to marry Alex. Didn't want a courthouse wedding. Didn't want lunch at Rocco's. Kate

71

didn't want white and didn't want anybody to be there except her and Alex. Audrey and Kate compromised on a shade of rose for Kate's dress, and Audrey, in a burst of generosity, got one of the designers at West Coast to make a pattern, then persuaded a stylish dressmaker in Beverly Hills to assemble the dress. "Thank you," Kate said as she stood in front of the dressmaker's mirror, amazed at the echo of rose in her face. Her breasts were full under the fitted bodice, and the slightly dropped waistline emphasized her hips.

She spilled champagne on the dress at the festive lunch, along with several fancy Italian sauces. The last thing she said to Audrey as the train left for Carmel and a weekend honeymoon by the sea was, "As beautiful as the dress is, I'm leaving it on the train. I'm never going to be a bride again, and I never want to think I could be." Audrey didn't object. Alex and Kate, in their compartment on the train, spent the next couple of hours drinking the cognac Alex had brought, giggling, taking the dress apart, seam by seam. One wedding dress. One marriage. One man. It was simple.

"Are you and Sheila going to get married?" she asks Mac.

"Sheila talked to you about that?"

"A little."

"Do you mind?"

"Mind? That's an odd word."

"I mean, do you care—do you—uh—approve of me?"

"Approve?"

"Yeah. Isn't that what people are supposed to do when their kids get married—approve?"

Kate laughs. Mac glares at her. She reaches for his hand and says, "I was thinking about Alex and me, when we got married, that's all. What does Sheila say?"

"She almost says yes."

"There's nobody I'd rather see Sheila marry," Kate says, telling the truth for this particular moment. Also hearing "almost," thinking, "People don't say 'almost' when they mean 'yes.' " Then she says, "Marriage is great," but she turns the photo of Alex upside down in front of her.

"You don't seem too happy about it right now," Mac says.

"Alex wants to spend time this summer trying to paint again."

"That sounds all right." Now she glares at him. He gets up to go into the living room where he left his camera on top of the piano.

Kate thinks, "Audrey's got a point. The kitchen could use a coat of paint." She and Alex painted these walls butter yellow one joyful weekend. The yellow is the color of dust now, catching grease and words, catching all that's gone on in this kitchen for years. Catching Kate with an ugliness she isn't used to seeing in her house, in herself.

The attic tomorrow: She'll confront the vague red and orange painting. Alex will have the pleasure of being the beginner, which carries such elation, so little sense of plain hard work. He'll have the rest of the summer to play with his paints and visit Sam. She'll go up to the attic to try to understand what's incomprehensible to her at the moment.

So Alex thinks he wants to paint. Does she want him

to? She closes her eyes against the yellow walls. She doesn't want to share art with Alex. She wants him in the background like the piano in the photo of Sheila. "Oh, please, let me be more generous than that." But she's not. She picks up the photo of Alex again but quickly puts it aside, turns to the one of herself on the proof sheet, moves it directly under the light. She can't tell what she looks like.

Sheila's been in her room all day, writing. Audrey went home after the crepes. Alex went to Sam's. Kate moved around the house without anything to do. Finally, she drove to a movie in the afternoon—a comedy she didn't find funny.

Mac hands her the camera and sits again in the chair across from her. He says, "You know why I decided to be a photographer? So nobody would take my picture." He smiles uneasily. "I'm in your hands."

She lifts the camera and focuses. The film, she knows, is black and white. "The best kind for the sudden deepening of those lines around his eyes." She recalls a painting by Albert Bierstadt of a bison, resting, its eyes not the small, mean eyes of buffalo, but the eyes of a creature that knows how much it weighs.

Mac keeps talking as she takes his picture, trying not to pose. "You know," he says, "my folks were divorced when I was seven and my little brother was five. My mom worked, and when she wasn't working, she had migraine headaches." He puts his elbows on the table, and Kate gets a head-on shot of him—all eyes and serious roundness. "I found out pretty fast that one person isn't a very good way to live. My dad came over every week to take Stubs and me to the movies and to stay all night with him.

74

Mom would hand us over, like a formal church thing, a ritual, with the same questions every single week, like, 'Have you got a dime to call me if anything happens?' She didn't trust him with us, even though we were his kids. Mistrust is the worst. Absolutely the *worst*." He pushes back on the squeaky legs of the chair. Kate's afraid he'll fall backward. She puts the camera down to warn him that the chair isn't very sturdy.

But Sheila has come down from her room and sneaks up behind him, gives him a shove to an upright position. He jumps, startled, gets up to hug her, but she pulls back, coy, and says, "What will Mother think?" She goes to the stove to boil water for a cup of tea.

Sheila's old pink chenille bathrobe travels with her to the stove—the robe she insists belonged to her muse hundreds of years ago. She fingers her green-marbled pen— the only one she can possibly write with—in her pocket. Words have been coming all day. Two men love her. She's so full of words that she can't talk now. Mac and Kate don't know about Ralph or her writing. She's sorry she made that dumb remark about What Will Mother Think, but she sees the photos spread out on the table. Kate courts Sheila's boyfriends. "Kate the Artist." This thought is as sharp as the strong mint tea she's about to brew.

Kate hunches over the photos, suggesting that Mac crop one to focus more on Audrey's face. "Hunched over like a lizard," Sheila thinks and becomes a bird aiming for the lizard. She pokes Kate in the ribs and tickles her. Kate can't stand it. Gets up. Faces Sheila and says, "Cut the foolishness. Just cut it out and make up your mind about what you're going to do this summer." She quiets her voice. "You and Mac would probably like some time together. I'm going to bed. Alex is at Sam's—he'll be home by eleven or so, he said. He has to be at the committee tomorrow morning. Audrey wants us to come to dinner at her house this week, so give that some thought." Without looking again at either Sheila or Mac, she heads upstairs to her bedroom. She has trouble falling alseep without Alex. When she does, she dreams of a river. She's forced into it by nothing she can see, but she is undeniably thrown into the current. "I can swim," she thinks in the dream, but weeds tangle around her legs.

Dear Kate and Alex,

I've been writing all day and most of the night about what shapes we take. Livia's line: "Every shape throws its sparks." About sparks that appear and disappear, about how people change.

The shape I've been to you is "daughter." A hope of some kind. I'm not your hope. You've known that since I was ten, or so you tell me. You've preached independence, but that has a certain meaning for you, a special beauty that you want to see in me. I'm not beautiful. I'm half-human these days, half-beast, half-warm, half-cold.

I haven't felt right since I've been home this summer. I guess it's because my element is changing from this house to deep water—from the past to diving into things. Independent? You say you don't want me to be safe, Kate, then you turn around and demand that I make some definite, safe decision about what to do with myself.

I've been stumbling. Today as I was writing, a bunch of books leaped off the shelf above the bed and almost did me in. Things jump at me. This bruise on my head isn't really an accident;

it's a deliberate reminder. I'm having a tough time. I'm not innocent, no matter how innocent I've tried to be since I've been home. I've wanted to be your daughter again and not make a fool of myself or hurt you. I asked you for help, Kate, with money and getting a place of my own. Then I told you about meeting the poets in Venice and about Mac. You said, "Trust yourself." Why is your advice always so good but never quite right for me? You're my mother. A fine person. I hate you for being such a fine person and such a fine mother.

Sheila's handwriting scrawls, the words growing larger and larger, which happens when she's afraid of what she's writing. She pulls the quilt from the bottom of the bed and shifts her notebook to balance it on the knees that were touching Ralph's knees this morning. "Run away with me," was the last thing he said to her as she ran toward her—her parents'—house.

She looks at her oversize ". . . such a fine mother." It's true. Kate has been so much better than most mothers. Bonnie's mother was such a bitch that she wouldn't give Bonnie money or any kind of help when she found out about Bonnie's drinking and the witchcraft. Bonnie had to leave college and get a job as a waitress for a while. Then she started drinking again. It will probably be like that for the rest of her life—a job for a few months, then drinking, then a hospital or jail, then a job. Kate hasn't used her power to abandon Sheila or make her feel worthless. "But Kate is too good. All that therapy she went through, all her devotion to painting." Sheila's eyes sting, but she doesn't know if she's hurt by Kate's strength or by her own inability to have a single clear feeling about

77

her mother. She wipes at her tears, then straightens the notebook in front of her.

I'm sorry, Kate. I'm sorry, Alex. I don't hate anybody. I hate the pretense that we're all so creative and admirable and smart and able to work things out. I want to tell you about things I couldn't work out.

As I was picking up the books that fell today, I found one you gave me, Alex, the day I came home with the news that I was going to graduate from high school with honors. You thought I was ready for adult wisdom, I guess—you handed me <u>Altars</u> by M. Setzer, dusty and loose at the binding, a book your Grandfather Levinsky bought you when you were in high school. The premise of the book, you told me, is that a verse in the Old Testament hints that God prays. I thought you were out of your mind to give me such a weird thing—me, the smartest person in the world, right? Who needs God's prayers? Especially translated by somebody who wouldn't even put his whole first name on the cover. The "M" looked like a cheat, and I wasn't so sure about God, either. But listen, I read <u>Altars</u> a lot when I was at S.F. State.

I had a roommate named Bonnie. You two never met her. She got drunk all the time. She was eighteen and constantly boozed out. Bonnie and—well, I've got to call my other roommate X, because I promised I wouldn't ever tell her name—advertised on a campus bulletin board for somebody to share their flat. I couldn't live in a hotel more than a couple of weeks into school that first year, and the dorms—nobody, but nobody, lived in the dorms.

I wrote to you about the Berkeley flat, but you never saw it. We each had a room, and we shared a kitchen and bathroom.

There wasn't any living room. There was, but it was Bonnie's. She'd found the place, so she got the biggest space. Usually she laid around, drinking whiskey. She ate a lot of Ritz crackers and potato chips and Fritos. We had good talks. I liked her. She never explained herself to me, never expected me to explain myself. I tried to get her to go to the clinic on campus, but she had plenty of money and plenty of excuses. "I'm not going to some cheap shrink," she'd say. She had a face like one of those photographs people take of what are supposed to be ghosts— fuzzy and unfocused, but human enough to make you think the dead do exist around us.

She was into magic and burned candles for spells. It was Santeria—Caribbean magic. I got interested because it sounded pretty practical. The bright candles enlivened the flat, and the chants and prayers had a peaceful effect on me. I'd heard about this from Ralph. His grandmother knew a Mexican version. She used herbs and spells for healing.

X was even more into magic than Bonnie and called herself a witch, which is why I can't tell her name. X didn't even pretend to go to school after the first few weeks. She fell in love with a man who wouldn't look at her. She spent hours—days— following him around, stealing little things of his, like cigarette butts out of restaurant ashtrays, to use in her love magic. Nothing was working. She asked Bonnie and me if we wanted to perform a huge love spell. We all had somebody we wanted to bewitch.

One night a couple of months before this love spell business, I left the flat to walk. I threw my coat over my bathrobe and prowled and worried about whether I'd ever be a writer. San Francisco State English classes were tough. The weather was cold. I shivered and worried and then decided that I'd show my writing to my English instructor the very next day.

79

Hank was a writer himself. He sat with me after class in a bar in the Stonestown shopping center next to campus. We drank burgundy and discussed Thomas Hardy. Finally, I got up the courage to pull one of my stories out of my backpack and hand it to him. I said something embarrassing like, "I have to know whether or not my writing is any good." I wanted to die, putting myself on the line like that. He looked at me hard. His eyes narrowed, but his mouth smiled.

He read my story while I gulped my wine and thought about how dingy San Francisco State was. The buildings were grimy gray-blue. It was like an urban housing development. And did it make any sense sitting in a cheap bar showing my writing to a man in a fatigue jacket and hiking boots?

When he finished reading, Hank said, "The girl is believable. The boy isn't. The description of the hotel is lively and fresh, but the street scene is a direct steal from a half dozen you can find in any high school anthology. The ending is just right." He smiled even more. He squeezed my hand as he gave me back the story.

I went home to the Berkeley flat and huddled up in bed, where I wrote a feverish story about Hank. The fictional name I gave him didn't disguise him, so I didn't show him that story. I let him see the next one, which was about the disappointments of Sol's life. I never knew Sol, but I'd heard his complaining in your reminiscences, Alex. I heard him curse in the piano music he left—I used to play it, remember? As I was writing the end of the story, I heard him wail, "They didn't even know I tried." I ended with that line.

It was Hank I wanted to bewitch. His interest in my writing— he loved the story about Sol—wasn't enough. Taking his class wasn't enough. The glasses of wine two or three times a week weren't enough.

One night Bonnie and X and I did the spell. We each took an herbal bath, and we each wore a gardenia in our hair—a powerful love flower. Bonnie'd been drinking all day. I had grass, so I smoked a joint. X said that booze or drugs gets in the way of the spirits, but Bonnie couldn't get along without liquor, and I was nervous.

We lit three green candles to St. Martha, who's supposed to conquer wild beasts. She dominates the love object so he can't rest until he comes to the person who's cast the spell. We started to chant. We went on for hours, very softly, very intensely. Just after midnight something came to us, but it wasn't St. Martha. There were two windows in my room—we'd decided to use mine because it was at the back of the flat and the most private—and both those windows cracked at the same time. The candles burned faster and faster, right down to the candle holders in seconds. The room was totally dark. The air got colder and colder. We could hear hooves against the hardwood floor. We were naked with the damn gardenias in our hair, in a room that was suddenly freezing and pounding. X leaped up and turned on the lights, told us to get dressed, to get out until she brought some sea salt. When she did, we sprinkled it around and said prayers X knew. The sea salt on the cold air smelled like dank caves in the mountains—and the smell stayed in the room afterward.

I spent most of my time in other places besides the flat during the winter. I didn't think I'd ever be warm again. I'd hang around the shopping center after classes, or I'd go back to Berkeley to a café called the Big Cheese and study. I'd sit in the back booth and eat cheese omelets and read Thomas Hardy or whoever Hank was throwing at us. I'd read a few pages of Altars because it gave me the feeling that if God could pray, so could I. I didn't feel so smart at that point. San Francisco State was very com-

81

petitive when it came to creative writing. I was trying to get good grades, and I'd signed up for too many units, thinking I could handle everything. Neither of you programmed me for failure. You two set me up for truth and beauty, not for waking up nights, exhausted from the school grind, in a foggy room with cracked windows, thinking I could hear something standing over my bed, something that smelled like sweaty, dirty fur.

Hank lived in Berkeley. He craved a cheese soufflé once in a while. He was writing a pessimistic novel—thirty-five years old and he thought he knew everything there was to know about a life based on fatalism. Maybe he did. I didn't.

The notebook slips. Sheila stops writing to bring it back onto her knees. How shall she say it? "I lost my virginity one winter night?" Skip that night. It was nothing. She was curious about how lovemaking looked. She'd never seen people make love. She couldn't take her eyes off of Hank's penis as it grew erect. Later, she couldn't stop looking at her own body to see if there was any difference. Hank was surprised that she was a virgin. She shakes her head, feels her hair around her shoulders. "Passionate hair," Hank said after that first lovemaking when he held her all night. She learned to make love. She learned to look forward to it, to stare at Hank during class and feel secret and proud that she knew what his body was like under his bulky sweaters, his corduroy pants.

She gets up from the bed, twists her hair on top of her head and pins it with hairpins from the top of the dresser. Alex's hair, but not quite. Kate's cheekbones, but not quite. "Half-Jewish, half-Christian," she thinks. "New York ghettos and midwestern lawns. Great-grandfather Levinsky and Audrey. Prayer shawls and sportswear."

She's been to Jewish temples and Methodist churches without understanding either as her own. She wants writing to be her religion, her life. At San Francisco State, the consensus was that nobody made a living being creative unless he was inside academia. Sol had had his wife and daughters to work for him. Kate has Alex. How will Sheila make a living and worship at the same time? Livia talked about being a typesetter, doing that part-time for money. She writes, works, can typeset her own books.

"Trust yourself." Finish the letter. It's almost 4 A.M.

Hank and I had a big affair. We were together for my first and second years of college. It was a movie—sensual special effects, colors and lights in the best places. I wanted to bring him home, but he'd say, "Families ruin love." He'd hug me goodbye at the bus station endlessly, like he was going to miss me a lot, and he'd whisper that we had a precious secret. Then he told me the spring of my sophomore year that he'd fallen for a freshman. She'd shown him a chapter of a novel she was writing; they'd had a few drinks together—it had just gone on from there, the way it had with me and with plenty of others.

I wasn't ignorant anymore. That was a blessing, wasn't it? I cried until that summer, wrote, made a few pretty good friends without Hank. But independent? Do you think I was ever independent? How could I be? There was always you. The night I locked my door when I was ten, I was testing you to see if you'd make me open it. I haven't locked my door since. I haven't had the nerve. I've wanted to depend on everybody just as much as I've wanted to escape.

I hope God is praying for us, if there is a God this summer.

Love,
Sheila

She lifts the pages she's written from the notebook. In a drawer of her dresser, she finds envelopes, stationery, a few souvenirs. On the bottom, there's sheet music—Bach exercises. Orderly harmony. She pulls it out, tears the sheets in half, and drops them in the wastepaper basket next to the dresser. So much for order. She sees, nestled in with the stationery, that one of the souvenirs she's kept is a small bag of dried herbs X gave her the last time they saw each other.

5

KATE, OPENING HER BEDROOM DOOR on Monday morning, feels the door resist. Sheila's letter, outside the door, is propped against it. She picks up the thick bundle sealed in an envelope, "KATE AND ALEX" in large letters on the front.

"A letter from Sheila," she says to Alex, who's rushing to get dressed. He puts on another gray shirt, this one a plaid of gray, brown, mauve. She sits down on the bed, weighing the envelope.

"Weren't you going to make me coffee? I have to hurry."

She doesn't want him to leave, wants him to sit next to her, talk about how they'll remodel the house this fall, repaint, then fix up the greenhouse for orchids. "Maybe we should read it," she says.

He takes the letter and balances it in his hand. "When did she write this epic? In the middle of the night?"

"Probably."

Midnight confessions. Alex can't take it. He tosses the letter onto the bed next to Kate and buttons his shirt.

She says, "I dreamed of a river last night. I kept going under, coming up, going under, coming up."

He wants his coffee. He gathers his wallet, keys, small change, his watch. It's too late for coffee. He mutters, "I dreamed of Grandfather Levinsky. He said, 'Redemption on earth, my boy.' What the hell does that mean?"

"Jews believe, don't they, that they can advance God's kingdom on earth through human effort? Maybe Grandfather Levinsky thinks this is your time to do something like that."

"Advance God's kingdom? Me?"

He puts a pen in his shirt pocket, all set to leave. Can't they talk about orchids? "At least take this and read it, will you?" She holds out the letter as he heads for the door. He sighs, grabs it, says, "After the committee meeting, I'm heading for Sam's. Don't fix dinner for me." He clatters down the stairs and out of the house.

Orchids. Delicate, easily torn, quickly browned at the edges. Kate aches for their sweetness, which lives on the efforts of a motherly gardener who mists them twice a day, steadies the blossoms with bamboo stakes, never lets a fragile head touch the ground. Kate used to take her dreams to a wise woman, a therapist. She remembers the smell of Lonnie's office as she'd push open the door every week. The sweet fragrance of modeling clay. Waxy crayons. Watercolors.

The office was a cluttered living room with a few soft chairs and a sand tray with little figures that could be placed in the tray to show a dream or inner situation. There was a clay statuette, a Greek sibyl, that Lonnie had sculpted. Kate hated to look at it, sensing something of her own dreaming in it—the burden of knowing more than one world. In their first meetings, she would tell Lonnie what she could recall of her dreams and cry with relief from the simple telling. Lonnie would ask questions. The dreams would begin to make sense as they talked. Kate dreamed once, during the early months of their work, of a dog pulling at a curtain that was drawn over a doorway. "Describe the dog," Lonnie had suggested, and when Kate did, said, "An Oriental guardian dog. You might try talking to it."

The dog said, "Sacrifice guilt," when Kate sat down with a sketch pad. Lonnie had said to write the dreams and then write associations to them, sketch them, talk to them. "Sacrifice guilt," Kate had written, amazed that this dream animal would enter her waking imagination and actually say something. She did a series of sketches of the dog. In time, she stopped crying when she saw Lonnie, sometimes didn't even talk much, would just show Lonnie what she'd been writing and drawing. Gradually, she became less of a stranger to herself. She never stopped being afraid to spend that hour with Lonnie every week and never stopped wanting to.

After three years, the dreams wouldn't budge. Kate couldn't go any further. "We're finished, then," Lonnie had said. Kate felt the way she had when Audrey announced, "I'm sorry, honey, your dad is dead." But this time there was healing, too. Lonnie stood up to hug Kate goodbye. Spring 1974. Kate walked out of the office, shedding the cardigan sweater she wore over her blouse. What a nice day. She went to a restaurant and ate a huge lunch.

As she makes the bed, she pulls up the flowing white bedspread. The river dream comes back to her, churning. That current pushed all night. She could use a guardian right now. She thinks of Jizo Bosatsu, a Japanese deity known for his compassion and attention to misguided souls. When she goes to the L.A. County Museum of Art, she searches out the carved wooden statue there of Jizo—Jizo in a monk's robe, kindly as Sam has never been. "A bath, breakfast, then out of the house."

Kate drives west on Wilshire Boulevard toward the museum, toward Jizo. In another building of the museum complex, there's a show of Russian avant garde art from the early 1900s. She'd like to see that, too. Later, she can buy a sticky bran muffin in the museum cafeteria, sit outside, feed crumbs to the pigeons.

Driving feels purposeful. She's weary of the sense that everyone is deliberately leaving her, that her family is disappearing, that her house is disappearing. But it feels right to be driving away from it, too. She crosses La Brea Avenue, looks south to where it stretches to the airport, north to the Hollywood Hills, then keeps her eye on Wilshire, driving carefully, knowing she's unsettled about Alex. Last night's episode with Sheila and Mac in the kitchen echoes.

At the La Brea tar pits, sculptures of prehistoric beasts hover above the black, bubbly tar. Nearby is the new Page Museum of fossils and prehistoric peoples. She loves museums as she loves libraries. The quiet, collected knowledge. Time to look at things until they speak to her in their own way. She can smell the museum before she gets to it—the cool, perfumed history of all the paint on all the canvases. Audrey once took her to the natural history museum in Exposition Park, which used to include the fine arts until this present museum was built. There were Daumier prints, grotesque exaggerations. At fourteen, Kate was amazed that an artist would dare to make statements like that. She was still engrossed in her black woman with the yellow dress.

Kate slows down as she passes the art museum. A large placard advertises the Russian show. She expects to see the usual street mimes and musicians—white faced clowns, flute players with their flute cases open in front of them for donations. But what she sees are black metal gates drawn across the sidewalk entrance. "Monday," she says to herself. "Of course. It's closed." A pickup truck honks behind her. She speeds up, turns the corner, pulls into an empty parking place on the street, and stops the car. Leans back, her head against the headrest. So. It's going to be like this. She should have kept Sheila's letter to read. She shouldn't have left the house without saying anything to Sheila, letting her sleep and leaving a note on the kitchen table. She should have remembered that the museum is closed on Mondays. She should have painted this morning, done her work, forgotten about escaping. No, it isn't escape she wants. It's solace.

The day Lonnie died, Kate was sitting in the backyard at home. Lonnie had been in a coma for five days from a brain tumor no one diagnosed until she collapsed and was rushed to U.C.L.A. hospital. Surgery was impossible. There hadn't been any hope at all. Kate tossed out peanut after peanut for the blue jays, thinking that if one of them would take a nut right out of her hand, there might be a miracle. It was a year after they'd stopped working together, but Kate and Lonnie had kept in touch, had met sometimes to have a glass of wine in the afternoon when Lonnie had finished with her clients and Kate could get away for a while before dinner. Once, Lonnie had said that more could be seen by looking at the back of a clay figure than by looking at how the artist shaped the front. The repressed truth came from behind. A blue jay flew close to Kate, closer than the smart and suspicious birds usually did, and she reached for it wildly. It flapped away, chattering. The phone rang. Lonnie's daughter, Zoë, said, "Leonora died an hour ago. You meant a lot to her. Will you come to the funeral and help me say goodbye?"

Kate had stood in the cemetery with twenty other people, hearing the unfamiliar name, Leonora. When Zoë spoke of her mother, she talked of dreams that go on in all the worlds at once. Kate wore a dress the color of the red wine she and Lonnie had shared on other afternoons. It was a spring day like the day she ate that big lunch after they'd said goodbye, but chilly. Near the end of the service, the wind came up and blew at Kate's legs. "Like the weeds of my dream last night." She stares out of the car window at the traffic threading the street. After the funeral, there had been food at Zoë's house. Zoë gave everyone something of Lonnie's. She said to Kate, "Take this. It may help," and handed her the sibyl that had stood in Lonnie's office, the sculpture Kate could hardly bear because it spoke to her of all the unknown. At home, she put it on the bedroom bookshelf where she keeps her

present dream notebook. The sibyl watches the room—
its sleep, its lovemaking—watches Kate dream. "I should
have stayed home today," she thinks again.

But she wants something that isn't at home. "I'll walk
down to the May Company and find a phone to call Audrey. Maybe she can meet me for lunch, or maybe I can
drive over and see her." She climbs out of the car, pulling
her cotton sundress away from the backs of her legs. She's
sweating. She slings her canvas carryall over her shoulder
and heads for the department store a block away. Cool air
rushes at her as its big glass door flies open.

Pink, gold, white, lavender. She's drawn to the colors
of the cosmetic counter. She sprays herself with cologne
from a sample bottle labeled "Fertility." The odor reminds
her of the herbs on her windowsill. In the greeting card
section, there are bunnies for birthdays; flowers for ill-
nesses; a pop art pickle with the message "Don't be sour—
write to me!" It would have been quiet with Jizo. There's
a pay phone behind the cards. She digs into her carryall
for a dime, remembers Mac's story about his mother giving
him a dime to call her in an emergency. "Is this an emergency?" she asks herself, slipping the money in the slot.
Audrey's phone rings. Audrey isn't exactly Jizo, but Kate
would like to see her. The phone rings on and on. She
hangs up. "Maybe I got the wrong number." She hadn't.
What now? Maybe she'll shop.

She wanders into the men's department. Fall clothes
are already out. A mannequin wears brown corduroy pants,
a gray and brown checked shirt. She likes to buy shirts
for Alex, picks up one from a stacked counter. No. She
walks along the aisles of the store. Panty hose and leotards

and tights. Slippers. Purses and sunglasses. A table full of fall sweaters. Would Sheila like a forest green one to take back to school? Would Kate like a rusty orange one for herself? She runs her hand across the soft wool. It's been awhile since she's bought herself any clothes. No. Not today.

The May Company is close to La Cienega Boulevard. She could drive there and see what the small art galleries are showing these days. Bob Hunt's gallery should be open today. Bob—has she seen him since her last show? He sold the white painting for her, but they had dealt with that over the phone. He's still got a couple of the white paintings in his back room. He thinks he can sell them, too.

The whole ground floor of the gallery is taken up with a construction of wood and metal, various shapes arranged to create a kind of architecture. Its impact depends on how the viewer develops, successively, a sense of the shapes. The wood is highly polished; the metal is grainy. She stops inside the door to take a long look. "I like the air in the work. You can't get space like that in a painting." She walks between the jutting shapes. "It leads you where it wants you to go. It's not as free as you think it is at first." She leans over to inspect the subtle grain of the wood, the rough texture of the metal. Not as much contrast there as she thought. It's clever, sophisticated. Not brilliant, but not junk.

"Ah, beauty and the beast!" Bob says, coming out of the back room office. "I hate this thing." He flings an arm toward the construction. "It's very big. That's its only value. You're obviously the beauty but looking rather tired, aren't you? Let me see." He takes Kate's hand and leads her to his crowded office, shifts a pile of papers from a chair to his already littered desk, and gestures for her to sit. He stations his chair directly in front of her. "Somebody ought to be taking better care of you," he says.

Bob, close up, has the broad face of a friendly doctor. His hair was prematurely gray; now it's a startling milk white. Kate is about to tell him how Alex is, how Sheila is, ask about his wife, Pat, and his two sons, to make this an old-friends conversation. Instead, she looks at the wall of the office and says, of the white painting there, "That was one of the last ones."

She and Bob had fallen in love in 1968. The paintings came after their affair was over, but she sees him in the canvas behind his desk, a snowy outline in the background outside of a white window. She reaches across to him and smoothes a loose strand of hair away from his face. 1968, 1969. Janis Joplin songs had gotten inside Kate, no matter how much she tried not to listen. And Gene's death in the Vietnam War. And her nutty mescaline poem. Bob couldn't tell her anything about the poem when she showed it to him, but he did talk for hours about Carlos Castaneda and about getting out of L.A. He admired her work, the first tentative paintings she did after the sketches of Sheila were finished, said she knew more than she thought about Other Realities. He mentioned auras—did she see them?

Sheila had locked her bedroom door against Kate's mothering that year. Alex was obsessed with making a living for them, which wasn't a living to Kate but a distance from her. The halting rhythm of trying to paint again after ten years was frightening. Whatever Bob saw in her work gave her hope.

"We'll camp out, all across the country," Bob would

say as they lay together in West L.A. motel rooms. "We'll buy a van, make pilgrimages to forests, wash in rivers, find a deserted shack for the winter." Then he'd look at her with the same humor and directness she sees in him now as she takes her hand away from his face. She sensed that his exuberance was Castaneda's, not his. Auras? No, she didn't see them. Bob was basically too honest to believe he did, either. They needed each other briefly, that was all. She wanted, she discovered, to go home to the messy strain and love of her family more than she wanted to fantasize about pilgrimages.

The last time they were together, she'd said, "We're kidding ourselves." They didn't make love but opened the ice chest they'd brought, sat on the bed and ate tuna sandwiches, drank apple juice. They talked about their kids and knew they'd ended something foolish.

But the deep, yearning reds of Kate's present paintings swim in her. She misses Bob as he was with her once. She misses Lonnie, too. Sometimes keeping track of her own dreams isn't enough. Sweat slides under her arms, down her sides, even though it's cool in Bob's office. She's forty-five years old. The white painting blurs in front of her. In that photograph of Mac's, she couldn't even tell what she looks like.

"Dear God, you are tired," Bob says, pulling her up, out of her chair. "Let's go somewhere."

Sheila wakes up at noon, stretches under the sheet, looks out the window. "It's hot again," she thinks. The bright houses sit heavily in the hills. She heads for the bathroom, wanting water through her hair and all over

94

her body. It doesn't take long—a shower and the hair dryer, Kate's bath powder under her arms, in her crotch, on her ass, across her shoulders. In her bedroom, she gets a favorite pair of white shorts out of the drawer and steps into them. "You fox, you," she says as she looks in the mirror with only the shorts on. She digs around in the drawer and finds a black top she likes that's just a line of fabric across her breasts.

Kate's note on the kitchen table says, "Gone to the museum. Home late afternoon. Let me know where you'll be. Love, K."

"Where will I be?" Sheila opens the refrigerator, takes out a bottle of orange juice, a package of flour tortillas, sharp cheddar cheese. She heats a tortilla on one burner of the stove, flipping it before it burns. Then she slices cheese and wraps it in the tortilla. Kate's gone. Alex is gone. No car. She was thinking she might go out to Venice. Livia gave her her phone number. It would take forever on the bus, for God's sake. Mac's at work. His proof sheet and the eight by tens are still on the table. A photo of her is circled on the sheet. She sees herself with an expression of surprise on her face that makes her look young, eager. After Kate had gone to bed, Mac wanted an answer. The young woman in the photo looks as if she'd like to get married. When Sheila's with Mac, she is this willing, kind, agreeable person who could marry a steady, tender young man. The wedding: white dress and black tux. A sugar bride and groom on top of the cake, sugary organ music.

"The cheese doesn't melt enough when you do it this way," she thinks. "I should put these things in the oven."

But she's too hungry to wait and fixes another tortilla on top of the stove. Ralph said yesterday—what was it?—about rehearsing? While they were in the greenhouse. About his group—oh, right—at the old Cuba Club down on Sunset this afternoon.

In the living room, she goes to the piano and plays scraps of the Bach exercises she tore up last night. "Easy and orderly," she thinks, but that doesn't last long. She moves into Latin rhythms. "No," she sings, "not Ralph." A crescendo. She slams both hands on the keys. Why not Ralph? Her letter to Kate and Alex was about taking risks.

A sugar bride and groom. A slice of wedding cake wrapped in aluminum foil, frozen, and saved for a first anniversary. A long satin dress mothproofed and preserved for the next forty years. Bank accounts. A budget. Letting somebody know where you'll be all the time, how much you spend, what you're thinking, what sizes you wear so the birthday and Christmas presents will fit. Weekly menus. Pet names. Favorite TV shows. Tune-ups for the car.

She lopes, sweating, her hair wet at the roots, down to Sunset to wait for the bus into Echo Park. She wants the cool shadow of a nightclub in the afternoon, a place that smells of last night's smoke and this morning's disinfectant. She looks along the street for the bus and sees a young woman she recognizes—always stoned, always with her jeans unzipped and her belly showing. She wanders to the bus stop, rubbing herself, looking at Sheila or not, Sheila can't tell, with dead-flower eyes. Is it Bonnie? Is it Sheila herself, waiting for the bus, already in trouble? Sheila senses her own bare legs. Ralph will see them the minute she walks into the Cuba Club. It's deserted in the

96

daytime except for the musicians who rehearse their music in the dark, who can see in the dark, too.

He does see her. She can't quite make him out. The light from the street is still in her eyes. There's the rasp of instruments being lifted out of their cases, the pop of electrical jacks being plugged in. She jumps at a sudden screech—the electric guitar, testing.

"Over here!" Ralph calls to her as he leaves the bandstand. They meet in the middle of the empty dance floor. She doesn't know him in all this darkness, yet she knows his arm around her: the arm from four years ago, from yesterday. He leads her to a table.

"We've got beer and we've got dope—you want anything?" She shakes her head, smells the disinfectant and, underneath that, the sour odor of last night's drunk. The piano starts a blues tune that she remembers: "Born under a Bad Sign."

"I'll just listen." For thirty minutes she absorbs the piano, trumpet, bass, electric guitar, drums. San Francisco. A club like this. A jazz group Hank wanted to hear. He said they could dance. But instead, he told her about the young woman who was taking Sheila's place. He left her at their table, saying, "You'll do fine, passionate Sheila, without this old crow." The crow rose from the table, paid the waitress, winged his way out of the club, out of her life. She stayed, told the waitress she'd like another drink. A man asked her to dance when the jazz got mellow, and she let him buy her even another drink, and by the end of the evening she was drunk with this stranger who had only asked her to dance. She was willing to love him in the backseat of his car, in the fog. She heard crows circling the car. They might get in, scratch her, claw at her eyes. She kept her eyes closed while the stranger struggled with her clothes and finally shoved himself into her.

The blues can take a long time to play if everyone gets a solo, if everyone wants to take another solo, if the afternoon is midsummer in the old Cuba Club, where Latinos have been coming for years, where jazz and mariachi and ballroom dance bands have played for years. "If it wasn't for ba-a-ad luck, I wouldn't have no luck at all." Sheila hears Ralph honk on his trumpet, then slide into eerie quarter tones. His playing vibrates. The floor shakes under her feet. As the blues ends with a low note from his horn, an extended tone that echoes all the way through her, she wants some grass.

There's a general hubbub on the bandstand. "Hey, man, that was *it.*" "We were really *cookin'.*"

Ralph slips into the chair next to Sheila. "How was that, babe?"

"Great. Do you want to smoke a joint?"

Danny, the drummer, comes to the table. He's heard an argument in the music between the bass player and the guitar player. "They just weren't cooperating, man," he says, his thin face worried. "It wasn't that they were off the beat, but they weren't with it, either. Those guys are gonna ruin a set sometime, you know?"

"Frank and Rudy have been at that shit for years. You know how they are. Forget it. You know Sheila, right?"

Danny nods. He knows Sheila. Sheila and music—that's all Ralph ever talks about. He gives her half a smile. He's still wearing his Dodgers cap.

98

"I like your music," Sheila tells him.

"Listen, let those guys slug it out on their own," Ralph says. "They love each other. They just can't stand each other."

Ralph has known these musicians since junior high. They were in a gang together, Los Shadows. They got out of trouble with their music. They were so good that even the teachers and principal had to forgive them for stealing hubcaps, stealing batteries, stealing the WASP girls from the WASP boys. Ralph had it all going for him until the gang started to steal cars, not just occasional parts. One Shadow got caught and sent to prison. That scared these guys—five musicians who wanted to play music, not go to jail. Nobody said "Los Shadows" much the last year of high school.

Ralph and Sheila get up. Danny moves back to the bandstand. "A couple of minutes, man," Ralph says.

"Don't get wasted!" Danny shouts. "We've got to rehearse!"

Ralph leads Sheila into the men's restroom and lights a joint. "We'll find a better place for the next one," he says, nodding toward the urinals and sinks.

"I don't mind." She takes the joint from him as soon as he lights it.

"You're so eager, Sheila." He whispers this, as if she's not supposed to hear it, but she does, closes her eyes, leans against the wall, takes three long tokes before she hands it back to him.

When they finish, he douses the roach. He puts his arms around her, kisses her, and she opens her mouth, pushes against him. She feels him, hard through his pants.

Too ready, too soon. He pulls away, rests against a sink for a minute, then they go back to the club, the music. She listens without thinking, without anything in her head at all, until late afternoon when Danny says, "That's enough. We gotta save some juice for tomorrow." A final race around his drums, and he stops playing.

Ralph kneels on stage to put his trumpet in its case. In spite of his excitement in the john, it doesn't feel perfect the way he thought it would to see Sheila here waiting for him, wanting to taste him and let him get her clothes off, finally get down to it. She's been his special, inner music. She was sweaty in the john and greedy with the joint. Her hair isn't like he remembered—there's so much of it, like those chicks who are too hip for their own good, trying to look intellectual and sexy at the same time. She looked great in the greenhouse. She looked great walking into the dim light of the club. But when he leaned against that sink, getting himself together, he'd seen her in the glare of the unshaded electric bulbs in the john. He sits on the edge of the bandstand and puts his head in his hands. She was his special, inner—

Sheila comes over. "What's the matter?" she asks.

What's he waiting for? She's here. He's got half a lid of sinsemilla in a plastic bag tucked in his sock. They can go somewhere and really fly. There's still a chance. There's got to be a chance. "Let's go," he says, pulling his head up.

Danny calls to him, "Tomorrow at noon, man! Don't forget. We've got to rehearse for the gig tomorrow night!"

"Tomorrow at noon," Ralph says.

6

THE LAVENDER RAIN of jacaranda blossoms spends itself on the porch of the house and on the ground below. As the blossoms die, they soften, oily and moist. They make no sound, dropping, dying. The house itself quiets in the early evening.

Kate's note to Sheila lies on the kitchen table along with the photographs. There's no answering note. The bottle of orange juice, forgotten, sits on the counter next to the sink. Kate's painting waits in the attic. The reds, in the evening light, shift on the canvas. The orange has faded again to the background. The figure at the bottom of the canvas is clearer in shadow than it was to Kate when she looked directly at it. It's Kate herself who emerges, not a mysterious figure, though the face is older and simpler than Kate's—a distilled face as silent as the house, as the jacaranda blossoms.

Coming in the front door, Kate feels the silence. Her favorite rocking chair stirs slightly, as if someone has just gotten up. Grandfather Levinsky. The old maybe-Persian rug rests in its pattern of flowers and domes. The couch relaxes in its usual place next to the wooden chest with candles on it.

She wants to look at her painting. As she and Bob sat all afternoon over lunch, she lingered as long as she could before they had to leave the restaurant, leave the temptation to be lovers again. But the painting was in her mind, its shapes merging and separating as she and Bob talked.

In the attic, she sits, takes off her shoes, leans back to look at her work. It's beginning to build. She sees herself. These red paintings—all the yearning, all the figures—are her. She smiles at the face on the canvas, says to it, "You want to be seen, do you?" She squeezes black oil paint from the tube onto her palette, works with the face until the eyes are the eyes that finally did leave Bob today, until the mouth is the mouth that insisted on breathing in the dream of the river, until the lines of the forehead are the lines that connect Kate to the woman she's becoming.

Mac's photo of her. She wants to see it blown up. Maybe it will tell her more about this new face.

Six o'clock by the kitchen clock. She calls Mac, who says, well, sure, he could print the picture from the negative tonight. "Is Sheila there?" Kate asks. No. "Alex isn't here. I don't know when either of them will get home. Come late, if you like."

She hangs up. She imagines Alex and Sam drinking warm saki, Sam holding forth about the value of living alone if you're an artist. Sam's wife left him because she couldn't stand his living alone, even when she was there. And Sheila? Kate starts to put the orange juice back in the refrigerator but passes the phone again and dials.

"Hello?" Audrey's voice, expectant.

"Hi. Can I come over for a while?"

"Kate? I was waiting for Flo to call. We thought we'd go out for dinner. Something different, like Greek food. Do you and Alex and Sheila want to come? I do want you all here for a meal this week, but maybe we could make a big deal out of tonight—out of every night! Now that I'm free—"

"I'd just like to be with you. I'm alone." Kate hears her own voice, low and tired.

"You're not going nuts, are you? All that therapy—you'd think you'd be more normal than normal."

"I'm not going nuts."

Audrey's on her white living room couch, stroking her Siamese cats, Ming and Flower. She's beginning to think that leisure isn't bad. Her Saturday night insistence on a plan for the future has quieted into "one thing at a time." She spent the morning reading a lush, historical novel, got a little itchy later and went out for an early lunch. She took her time eating the pastrami on rye, and her stomach felt fine. No more twenty minute lunch hours at her desk, trying to chew and dictate to Midge at the same time. Ming takes a quick nip at her hand to let her know he's had enough petting. She moves him gently off her lap. Flower follows him. They both lie, purring, on the thick white carpet at her feet.

Kate doesn't often ask to see her. She's flattered, in spite of her suspicious question about sanity. She sighs and looks out through the big window across the room. The roses in her garden are opulent this year. The aphids have capitalized on the abundance, though, and that spray Audrey's been using isn't killing the bugs; in fact, they're multiplying. How did she work and tend her roses all those years? She could spend hours every day in the garden.

Prince Charming might be waiting in the Greek restaurant tonight. She's never made love with a Greek. Are they really violent? She stretches her legs out on the couch.

"Audrey?"

"I'm here, just thinking about what we can work out for tonight." She's certainly not going to meet any man with her forty-five-year-old daughter sitting beside her. How could she even imagine it? Pickups in a restaurant. Cheap. "You want to eat at that health food place—the Natural Nosh? A cool salad? I'll see if I can get Flo, if you'll get off the phone. Come on over."

Kate's voice drops even lower. "Thanks, Audrey."

" 'Thanks, Audrey'?" Audrey thinks, hanging up. "In that voice? What's with her?"

Audrey calls Flo, who says, "Tell Kate hello and be nice to her, Aud, for heaven's sake."

"I am nice to her."

"Try to approve of her. You didn't even invite her to your retirement party. Were you afraid she'd show up naked or what?"

Audrey, in her bedroom, opens the closet where her clothes are arranged by color and season. She checks the mirror on the closet door. "Not bad," she assures the mirror. She still has a womanly figure. She's pleased with her looks. "Except my face. You can't do a thing about wrinkles—I don't care what magic potions you buy."

Ming comes in to see what's going on. She picks him up, his soft, clean fur against her body. "If I can feel as good as I've felt today, I may never have another ulcer attack," she tells him. She picks out a brown blouse and plain beige skirt. As she smoothes the skirt over her hips, she remembers the feeling of her pink uniform, the one she wore to the drugstore. Kate's face, a child, comes back to her. "Always looking at pictures as if she could see to the inside of them. Art. Does it do anybody any good?" Those white paintings of Kate's that are selling now. How could anyone paint nothing but white like that? Yet they aren't nothing. There's something in them that makes Audrey think of Roy's funeral, even though she resists the thought. His coffin sliding into empty ground. That day, she hoped nobody would see her face under the black veil. She'd been taught to get through hard times with dignity.

"Art isn't dignified," she decides. She stands at the large living room window opposite the rose garden, surveys the houses on her block. This neighborhood is Los Feliz, just north of Silverlake. Los Feliz is affluent, conservative. A Cape Cod cottage painted blue sits on its own small hill. Bougainvillea, neatly trimmed, graces the doorway of John Elliott's Shakespearean two-story. She wishes the Mortons, next door to John, would get rid of the tacky plaster lions, one on each side of the entrance to their white Colonial. Ming and Flower pad across the carpet to her. "You can prowl tomorrow," she says, "but I don't want you out after dark."

105

Two musical tones of the doorbell. Kate's sundress is limp. That shoulder bag has seen better days. Oh, Audrey supposes, it's all right for the Natural Nosh. She supposes Kate's all right, too, as she gives Audrey a hug and says, "How's the lady of leisure?"

"Better than I expected. What about you?"

"I was out most of the day. Saw Bob Hunt at his gallery." She flops on the couch, admires the vase of fresh lavender roses on an end table. The white expanse of carpet is spotless. Kate notices black paint under her fingernails. Her sundress smells of the whole day's perspiration. Well, so she'll mess up the perfection a little.

"Do you want a drink?" Audrey asks.

"Sure, if you're having one."

Kate takes a long drink of her scotch and water, sinks into the fat pillows. "Did you know that Bob and I had an affair once?"

Audrey, settling herself on the other end of the couch, wonders if she really heard that.

"How many affairs have you had?" Kate asks.

"Please! We're mother and daughter!"

"What better people to talk about love? We're old enough."

"Old enough to know better." Audrey wants to kick Kate's canvas bag, that cheap thing. It slumps on the floor next to the couch, ruining the effect of the whole room. Then she looks at Kate's hand around her glass. The veins protrude. The skin is rough from paint remover. "We certainly are old enough," she thinks, looking down at her own well-manicured but thick-veined hands. "Twice," she says carefully, "there have been men I've—men I've liked a lot."

106

"You never wanted me to meet them?"

"It was none of your business. They were people I met working. One was around for a couple of years. Another one—off and on for a while. But—"

"But?"

But. Audrey would enjoy herself, then wouldn't be enjoying herself anymore. She'd get bored. Bored and scared. Afraid that she'd get past the boredom and into love. "I'd get tense," she says. "There wasn't enough room in me for a man and a job. Roy was, your father was—" Kate can know her own mother loved her own father, can't she? "Roy was the one man I really loved. He died. I suppose your therapist would have made something out of that."

Kate holds out her glass for a refill. "The white paintings were about Bob, but about Alex, too. And Sheila," she says. She tells her mother the story of the day in the kitchen when she wanted to commit suicide. Audrey lets herself remember Roy's funeral.

After another drink, Kate asks, "Can you take any more?"

"I can take a lot," Audrey says. The Rock. But now she fills with the crying she didn't do at Roy's funeral, the crying that started in her when she told Kate about retiring, the crying that almost burst when she hugged Sheila in the kitchen over the crepes.

Kate talks about Alex and his need to paint, his not being home, about Sheila and the friction between them. She talks about the painting in the attic. "This afternoon, I saw myself in it. Finally. I thought it might be you at first."

"Oh, God, don't paint me!" Audrey gets up to pull the drapes across the two big windows. It's night. "It's silly

107

to go out," she says. "We can rummage around in the refrigerator."

They eat cold, spicy chicken breasts, then creamy papaya that Audrey slices over the sink and hands to Kate without bothering about plates. Kate lets Audrey feed her and then go off on a meandering reminiscence about the first time they ate papaya in Los Angeles. They didn't know any fruit could be that sweet. "You know, Flower eats papaya—" Audrey picks up a bit of the fruit and calls, "Flower, Flower," but the cats are beneath the dressing table in the bedroom, asleep.

In another hour, after Kate is gone, Audrey will sit at the dressing table and smooth aloe vera cream on her face, thinking, "At least I'll have soft wrinkles." She'll get into a lacy nightgown, relax into her queen sized bed, turn on her side, reach across the bed to run her arm over the sheet where a man might lie, feeling his shape where there is no shape.

By eleven, Kate's on her way home. She phoned Mac from Audrey's. He'll meet her at the house; the photo is great—she'll love it. She drives slowly, the car windows down to catch the rich scent of the neighborhood's star jasmine.

She eases onto her own street, past the Horseleys' caramel stucco, the Watanabes' yellow cottage. It was a good evening with Audrey, just what she needed. The houses sit in the light of a moon that's just past full, beginning to show its lopsided phase, going down into darkness. As she pulls into her driveway, she sees that Alex's van is still missing. She didn't leave any lights on; it was daylight when she left for Audrey's. She'll have to be careful not to slip on the oily jacaranda blossoms. On the porch, she stops and listens. Something's different. She waits but doesn't hear anything unusual. "This afternoon's silence, simply deepened," she thinks. The door opens quickly with her key, and she walks into the house, glad to be home, until she turns on the light and gasps.

Couch pillows thrown to the floor. Rug jumbled and askew. Piano music strewn everywhere. Candles dumped off of the wooden chest. One front window jimmied open, pried up.

Locking the door, locking the car, putting a locked gate in the fence. They thought the house would be safe. So many years without any real trouble. It's stood through every meal, every flush of the toilet, every climb up the stairs, every newspaper thrown against the porch, every lighted candle that could have set the house on fire. Frightened, she steps into the room. The portable TV is missing from the shelf behind the couch; so are the stereo components.

"Are the thieves still here?" she wonders. Silence. She slides her hand along a fierce, ugly gash on the piano, then, shaking, touches the strings to see if any are broken. Theft. Breaking and entering. An invasion of privacy. Kate knows the words for what has happened, but not the real name for this. She plays a loud, dissonant chord on the piano, then puts her head down on her arms. If she'd been here, would they have come anyway? Or would they have seen lights on and known she was home, skipped the house and gone to someone else's? "Forgive me," she says out loud to no one.

"Kate?" It's Mac, photo in hand. "God, what happened?"

"A break-in." She lifts her head. "Just walk through the rest of the house with me, will you?"

The study is untouched. The kitchen looks all right. "They probably headed for the bedrooms," Mac suggests, "to steal jewelry or money."

Kate goes ahead of him into her bedroom. "It's chaos," she calls to him. "Wait for a second while I get my bearings." Three empty beer cans on top of the dresser—the wet bottoms have left white rings on the polished finish. Everything has been yanked out of the dresser drawers, and, at her feet, in the middle of one of her silk scarves, is a lump of human shit. She stoops, nausea at the back of her mouth, collects the lump in the scarf, carries it out of the bedroom and down the hall to the bathroom. "Go on in," she says to Mac, moving past him. She flushes away the whole mess. A stranger, shitting in her bedroom.

Mac is surveying the disorder when she comes back. The bedclothes are jumbled, books and paraphernalia from the bookshelf have been pushed across the floor, the clothes from the closet are spread across the room. Near her on the floor, Kate finds two tiny, round pictures of Audrey and Roy, cut out carefully one Christmas by Roy. They were in Kate's childhood locket, a locket of rosy Black Hills gold, the only thing she had that Roy had given her. On her knees, she searches through the mess, but the locket is gone. She crawls into broken clay. The sibyl. Its head and torso lie in front of her; the lower half is on the other side of the room.

Mac doesn't know what the statue is. He doesn't know

110

why Kate is crawling around, crying over some pieces of clay. "Aren't there people who do art repairs?" he asks. "Can't it be fixed?"

She tries to fit the pieces together, but too much has been shattered. Holding the rough-edged shards, she wants to vomit. "Who did this?"

"Gang kids, probably. They don't like nice houses, things people have worked for. They think everybody should be as dumb as they are."

"My painting." Kate stumbles out of the room, up to the attic. The face in the painting, her face, is beginning to settle and dry. Thank God. "It's okay," she says, coming back down.

"You want this?" Mac holds out the photo.

"I'll put it with the painting. I want to look at them together." She makes another trip to the attic.

Mac walks into Sheila's bedroom. The same thing here. Bedclothes thrown around. Books and records all over the place. Closet door open. He leans over to pick up a couple of books, put them back on the shelf. He's never read these—poetry by Sylvia Plath, *Mrs. Dalloway* by Virginia Woolf. Books from college. Things he doesn't know. Sheila reads these. Sheila writes. Things he doesn't understand. He holds the books and wants to set them on the shelf but can't get past how she can read and write things he doesn't understand. Friday night out in Venice, he saw how excited she got about those poets. He caught the drift of the poetry—that was about it. He sure didn't get whatever Sheila got.

Kate's shocked when she enters the room, can't believe that her daughter's room has been torn apart, too. Call

Alex. "We'd better leave it alone," she says. They go downstairs together, feeling old, older than Kate in her painting, older than Mac has any reason to feel, older than the house itself, which has said nothing, hasn't offered any clue to the intrusion, to the people who came here and took what they wanted, whether it made any sense or not.

"I'm going to call Alex," Kate says. Mac has already put on water for coffee. "How dare you?" the voice in her said all those months she wanted to die or leave the house or walk through the windows in her white paintings. "How dare you leave life, whatever it brings?"

What can she possibly say to Alex? "The house" is all she can think of. "Our house." She wants a long, hot bath.

"Where's Sheila?" Mac asks, measuring the special Cuban coffee into the basket of the drip coffeepot.

"I don't know."

"Has she seen Ralph this summer?"

"We ran into him at the Trails the other day."

"That lazy asshole! She said she never wanted to see him again, but she did. I knew she did." Mac grabs the boiling water from the stove, pours it over the coffee, barely avoids splashing it on himself. "I'll kill him!" he explodes.

"Stop it." Kate wants that bath. Mac has turned his back to her. His shoulders heave.

"I'll come home from Sam's right now," Alex says. "I'm sorry—God, I'm sorry. I should have been there. Hold on. Don't move anything. Have you called the cops? No. Okay. I will. Don't do a thing. I'll be right there."

There's a fine dust of powder left on the floor of the

112

bathroom from Sheila's shower this morning. Kate wipes it up with the sponge from the side of the tub. She runs her bath, adds bath salts, gets into the water before there's really enough to sit in. She eases against the still-cool tub, feels the water gradually move upward, slowly, until she can lean back. Finally, it covers her shoulders. She closes her eyes.

Alex, home, waits on the bed. The policeman on the desk said, "A car will be there as soon as possible." That could mean half an hour or the rest of the night. He's tried to straighten the bed but can't make head or tail of it, so he simply sits in the confusion of sheets and blankets. He and Sam spent most of the evening without talking. Alex made a few sketches—spontaneous things on a large pad of paper Sam lent him. The paper began to sing. He told Sam, thrilled, that he was going to stay forever, live with him until he learned how to be an artist again.

Alex makes another attempt to pull at the blanket that's uncomfortably jumbled beneath him. He can't get it straight. The sibyl is broken, he sees, and picks up the parts, tries to fit them together. No use. When he had finished drawing, he got Sheila's letter from his van where he'd left it. He read it through fast, wanting to get it over with. Then he read it again, slowly.

Kate finds him, his hair mussed, his hands puzzling over the sibyl, his shirt—so fresh this morning—wrinkled and sticking out of his pants.

"Kate?"

"Yes, it's me." There's nothing she can say to him or even to herself. She dresses, then paws through the mess for her old cardigan sweater. It was in one of the drawers. She discovers it, almost hidden under the dresser.

113

Sheila's letter has been tossed onto the piano bench downstairs. Mac dozes on the couch. Kate takes the letter into the kitchen. Alex has read it—the envelope's been opened. As she reads it, she realizes that everything that's happened in these strange midsummer days is happening to kill the past. None of them will ever feel the same about each other again. She remembers that little book *Altars*. A lot of God's prayers were for mercy. He asked himself to have mercy on human beings. She pulls the sleeves of the sweater down around her wrists. It's cold now, a contrast to the hot, smoggy day. "Los Angeles," she thinks, pouring herself a cup of Mac's coffee. "It's supposed to be paradise."

The police arrive. The blond one says, coming in cautiously, "What's the trouble here?" Kate wants to say, "Everything," but Alex just says, "We've been robbed." He leads them through the house. They dust for fingerprints; they ask questions. They fill out a form, say they'll get in touch if they have any information, to call them if they find anything else missing. The black cop says, "We've been seeing this for several months in your area. Three teenagers, it looks like, but we can't identify them yet. They're pretty violent—killed one couple's dogs. Don't worry—we'll get 'em." He smiles, and Kate realizes how truly young he is, not much older than Sheila and Mac. "Good night," he says, "and thank you for your cooperation."

"We can clean up tomorrow," Alex says, heading upstairs, his shoulders dropping as he goes, as if he's been holding them up by an act of will.

"Thanks for staying," Kate says to Mac, who woke up when the police arrived. They go into the living room and pull the rug back in place. Kate tries to organize the sheet music, but the titles blur in front of her tired eyes. "I'm going to bed," she says, giving up.

"Hey, Kate, I'm sorry, you know? I mean it. This has been tough on you. I didn't mean to blow up about Sheila before. It's just that she's hot one minute and cold the next to me." He shrugs apologetically. "You're a—hey, you're a terrific person. You've helped me. I never really said thank you." He escapes before Kate can respond.

Sheila and Ralph pull up in Ralph's rebuilt '54 Chevy. Sheila gets out, says, "Don't walk me up to the house— it's late." The car squeals away from the curb. She walks to the porch toward Mac. She doesn't see him until she's in his arms, then tries to push past him, but he holds her. The white shorts. The flimsy top. Ralph's car.

"Your house has been broken into."

"You're kidding!"

"No. Things are all right. At least with the house. Not with you and me."

"I guess not."

"How was it with Ralph?"

"Not very good."

"Do you want to talk about it?"

"No."

"Do you want to marry me?"

"No."

"Do you want to marry Ralph?"

"No."

It is past the middle of the night, the changing from one day to the next. In myth, Night is the daughter of Chaos. Now, Night's sons, Sleep and Death, part. The most dangerous moment has passed. Sleep and Death have gone in separate directions. At 3:00 A.M., the sleepers in Los Angeles turn in their individual dreaming. The moon, lopsided, is in Scorpio—a brooding sign. But even scowling, the moon is sensitive, and there are many dreams.

Sheila tumbled into her disheveled bed without inspecting the mess. She'll look at it all tomorrow. She only noticed that the sheet she pulled around her smelled of cheap perfume. The odor would frighten her if she weren't exhausted. She'll think about that tomorrow, too—the exhaustion, the evening with Ralph. Her last evening with him.

Past the middle of the night, and Sheila turns in her bed, dreaming of herself. She stands outside a circle of children. Her first crush, a little boy in a plaid shirt, asks her name. "But you know me!" she cries, pushing toward the circle. She can't get into the game they play, which she's played herself, many times. She gives up, helpless, and discovers that she's walking in a garden. There are plants to be watered—overgrown ferns, gasping birds of paradise with their orange and purple head-like flowers. It's her job to save the garden. She will, she promises herself. She will. She turns away from the smell of China's cologne.

China, fifteen, was with Creeper and Lucky when they broke into the house tonight. Thin and eager, China had thrown herself onto Sheila's bed, begging Creeper to get it on, to fuck her right here, right now. She took off her blouse and tried to grab him as he walked past her to see what they could steal from Sheila's closet. The boys were stumbling with flashlights, too nervous to think about

116

getting it on with China, angry at not finding cash in the house—why don't people keep some money around? They won't get anything for the TV, the stereo, or the tape recorder they find in Sheila's closet. "Let's go, let's go," the boys whispered furiously to China, who put on her blouse, felt to be sure Kate's locket was still around her neck.

She likes the locket, twists it against her skin now as she sits with the boys at Lucky's. His mom works the night shift, and his dad is out drinking. Even if Lucky's dad does come home, he'll be drunk and not even wonder what they're doing, sitting here, waiting until they can get the stuff that's out in the car to Señor Blankface, who gives them nothing, fuckin' nothing, for all the risks they take. But China loves to steal. She loves the locket and wishes she'd even brought the little pictures that she scratched out of it. Somebody's stupid family pictures. Man, she'd like to have those to show off at school when she goes back, if she goes back to that prison with its shit-faced teachers and boring classes. Maybe she won't go back. It's nobody's business how much white eye shadow she wears, the eye shadow that makes her feel mean and pretty and really somebody—somebody who can steal and get what she wants anytime she wants it, except for Creeper, who only fucks her when *he* wants to. They should be fucking right now. Maybe she can get Lucky to go get hamburgers. After all, it's his house. He ought to get them some food. But Lucky and Creeper are watching the late movie on TV, smoking Alex's grass, rolling on the floor and laughing about the shit they leave in people's houses, trying to figure out how much all that shit weighs, how it would look in one big pile with the dead dogs on top of it. Lucky pulls his switchblade out of his pants pocket and flips it open. "This has done some damage," he says, standing up, walking unsteadily toward China. "Get away from me, man," she growls, "and get me a burger and fries. Let me have some of that dope, too." She reaches for the joint that Creeper is holding.

The two young policemen stop at an all-night doughnut shop. "Not bad," the blond cop says, "no murders tonight." The black one nods, tired but alert as a banged-up car pulls into the parking lot. An elderly couple gets out and comes into the shop—that's all, just a nice old couple who can't sleep tonight.

The beach at Venice, far from Silverlake and Echo Park, is empty except for a few winos who have settled on the sand to sleep and for the sound of the tide, pulled by the moon in Scorpio. The poets Sheila admires rest in their apartments, dreaming of the ocean, of sea life emerging from the deepest part of the psyche. One dreams himself in the center of the ocean, held and supported by the water. Death and Sleep, moving apart, leave the beach to the coming light.

Kate dreams that a twenty-year-old is dying. The young woman has Kate's hair, fine and wheat colored, which she crops shorter and shorter. As she dies, she cuts away all that she's believed in. Kate watches her, grieving, then shifts in bed as Alex turns to his own dream: a wall that he has to climb, though he resents its bricks, its solid facade, the lack of toeholds or a stairway to make the climb easier. The wall is too high for him.

They won't remember these dreams. They will wake

up thinking only of cleaning the house and starting over, if it is possible to begin in the middle of things.

Past the darkest time. Audrey will not remember Roy appearing in her dream, soothing her, rubbing her back as he did years ago, saying, "We won't grow old together, but you won't grow old alone." She reaches unconsciously for a masculine shape next to her. The odor of roses.

7

X'S DRIED HERBS were spilled by the thieves as they rummaged through Sheila's drawers, then got mixed with gritty fingerprint powder the police left behind. Sheila, on her hands and knees, scrubs at the sticky fingerprint goo that fell on the hardwood floor. She's put away her books and records, changed the bed linen. When she finishes the floor, she'll straighten the closet. "Then I'll find a job," she tells herself.

"We're music," Ralph said in the motel room they went to after his rehearsal, but they'd left all the music in the Cuba Club. Love. A fantasy. The real thing was too real. She soaps and rinses, ashamed. Ashamed, even, of the floor, where so much of her life was tossed by the thieves. Her clothes, her journals, the herbs—everyone, from the intruders to the police, saw everything. She sees herself: a young woman who hasn't been able to make up her mind.

She could have used the mop, but Alex and Kate have it in their room. It feels better, anyway, to be down here, her knees pushing into the floor as she scrubs. She dreamed of—what was it?—plants needing water? The ferns at the edge of her mind disappear too quickly for her to remember, but soaking the floor is a relief, feels like the right thing to do.

Finally, it's clean. As she goes through her closet, she discovers that the thieves missed her portable typewriter. Her tape recorder is gone, though. "Oh, well, I hardly used it." She collapses on the bed. In the case with the tape recorder there was a tape of Hank reading her story about Sol. Hank had been feeling dramatic one evening. After the story, there was a conversation between them on the tape about what people like Sol can struggle for but never succeed at.

Ralph's limp penis. Sheila's tense legs. They sat on the motel bed, smoking grass, talking as they had in high school, in the greenhouse on Sunday. "We're music," he whispered, but their desire disappeared as soon as they took off their clothes. They should have made love four years ago. Or never. Their nakedness wasn't as thrilling as saying hello in the Trails' parking lot. "Re-creating passion is for novels, not for real life," Sheila mumbles into the bed. They touched and petted and tried to make love, until she couldn't stand the odor of Lysol and marijuana in the cheap motel room and had to get dressed.

She won't go back to school. Something in the dream she can't remember told her not to go back to anything. She weeps over the missing tape. Hank's voice. Love, entanglement. So damn sweet.

She lets it all go. Tears. Blood—she started to menstruate this morning, is glad to be flowing, to feel her own blood move. It's time to take care of herself. The tape doesn't mean anything. All she did when they talked was say, "Right," or, "Oh, wow, I didn't see that as I was writing the story."

Livia told her that typesetters make seven dollars an hour. Maybe she could learn to do layouts, too, and make extra money at that. But when would she have time to write? She should call Livia and talk it over.

"There are possibilities," she thinks, sitting up, wiping her eyes with her arm, propping three pillows behind her. Outside, the hills look soft, seem to melt in the heat. She opens the window, wide, then leans back, pushes her sweaty hair up on her head.

Maybe Kate will still give her money to get a place until she can earn some of her own. Maybe she can find a roommate—maybe Livia. She doesn't even know Livia. If she gets a job fast—but she doesn't know how to set type or do layouts—it would take a while to learn. "I'd better go to an employment agency and get a clerical job," she decides. She picks up her journal and makes a list.

What I want: (1) an apartment of my own, (2) enough money to live on, (3) a chance to be with writers and do my own writing, (4) a friend.

A friend. There's Janice, who dated Danny Lopez. Sheila always liked her. She's a nurse now. She'd probably talk about salt-free diets and kids with cancer. Toni? She lives out in the Valley. She was one of Hank's adoring students.

Sheila's going to have to call Livia. Today. She's tired, though, from driving around with Ralph half the night, saying goodbye to Ralph. After they left the motel, they got a chili dog. Then they drove and drove, looking for a movie they wanted to see. Nothing appealed to them. They ended up at a coffee shop on Hollywood Boulevard, a place with a lot of guys hanging around looking for women or for men, looking and looking. Sheila stared into her coffee, black and greasy, and didn't drink it. When Ralph finished his, they drove around again. They couldn't make love, but they couldn't leave each other yet.

It got late. They parked on a street near Griffith Park by the huge trees with gray, elephant-hide trunks. Sheila wished she could sit in one of them, way up in the branches, be alone for a long time. Ralph put his arm around her, a repetition of their old ritual. Now she'd seen him naked. There wasn't anything left to see, to feel, to wonder about, to be tempted by. His arm grew heavy; her shoulder ached under it. She was cold in her flimsy black top and skimpy white shorts. She said, staring into the trees, "It's all in the past." He looked out the window on his side of the car and said softly, "Shit." Then he took his arm away and started the car. She pulled her arms around herself. When he stopped the car, all she could say was, "Don't walk me up to the house—it's late." She wanted to say, "I love you. But love doesn't work for us. I hope God takes care of you, because we can't take care of each other." When she bumped into Mac on the porch, she wanted to run back to the car before Ralph could drive off. To say it.

It's too late. Too late for Mac, too. She should apologize to him. Good, big, sensible dude. Not yet. He'll be furious and self-righteous. She pushes herself off the bed, picks up the scrubbing gear and heads downstairs. Kate and Alex

123

haven't said anything about her letter. Alex looked wiped out this morning. Kate seemed okay, even happy. Sheila dumps the dirty water into the kitchen sink, sets the pails on the service porch, takes in the backyard: the fig tree and lemon tree, the old lawn chairs, the greenhouse and the garage. The jacaranda is shedding, just like the one in front. When she played Batman and Robin as a kid, the jacaranda was her headquarters for the Forces of Good.

Alex comes onto the service porch with the mop. "Hi," he says. They stand together and look out at the yard. "I thought I might paint in the garage. It won't take much to clean it up." He seems to be talking to himself, not to her, but she says, "I thought you were spending time at Sam's these days."

"Last night changed my mind."

They drift to the yard, sit slightly apart in two of the lawn chairs. Alex faces the garage, runs his hand through his sweaty hair, damp from mopping. Sheila's grateful for the shade of the jacaranda. "Did you read my letter?" she asks.

He doesn't turn away from the garage, but the expression on his face changes from his tired, cleaning-things-up look. Sheila hasn't noticed the nearly black shadows under his eyes before.

"Sure," he says. "Twice." Then he launches into a rehash of the break-in.

"What did you think about my letter?" she insists.

For a minute, she thinks he's going to go on talking about who the intruders might be, what they stole, how he should have been at home so it wouldn't have happened, but then he says, "I thought of you in San Francisco in

124

your jeans and a nice white sweater, studying all the time. I always imagined you on campus. You had a serious, scholarly look about you. Your letter made me give up that innocent vision."

She tells him that her tape recorder's been stolen along with the tape of Hank reading her story. "I loved that story," she says, "but I don't now. I want to write what I don't know how to write. Every time I get stuff on paper, I see Hank's face, frowning. He corrects my language, makes all the 'right' suggestions." Jacaranda blossoms fall, crowd her chair. She picks up a few, then lets them drop through her fingers. "There's a mysterious woman who's following me around in my head. Not the muse of my old bathrobe. Nobody I recognize. She wants me to write for her. I tried on Sunday. A long thing, rambling on about sparks and shapes and the future. It's no good. When I saw it sticking out of my journal this morning, the pages crumpled on the floor, I knew that was right. All crumpled words, nothing fresh. Still Hank's influence. I don't know how to write for a new muse."

Alex angles his chair closer to hers. "I'm forty-five. I've got a catch in my back that kills me sometimes. I don't know if I can stand at an easel for even an hour. I haven't made a painting since you were six months old. My bed was so messed up last night that I couldn't get the sheets straight." He stretches his long legs toward her and touches her toes. An old Alex joke, tickling her toes with his. "Sam's clear about everything. It's easy to think I can work again when I'm around him. The test is whether I can do it by myself."

In 1971, the year Kate fell silent, Alex often took Sheila

to the movies or out for ice cream. He winked at her behind Kate's back to let her know things were all right, even if they weren't. He put flowers on the kitchen table. Sheila would see a vivid bouquet of daisies or mums and feel normal, although her mother was lying down most of the time, wouldn't talk, sneaked out to the garage to paint white, white, white. "Can't Kate help you?" Sheila asks.

"Oh, darling, you are young. The person you help is usually the one who can't help you at all."

"But you and Kate—"

"I know. We've been together for a lot of years."

"I told Mac last night that I didn't want to marry him. I can't forget his face, like a stray animal that doesn't understand why somebody won't give it a home. I can't get away from loving Ralph, but I don't want to see him again. Men admire my hair and legs and think I'm what they want, which makes me want them. They talk to every part of my body but not to me. I can't give anybody anything anymore."

"Grandfather Levinsky used to say, 'God loves the man who gives—' " Sheila finishes the old saying, " '—but doesn't give more than God himself would.'

"I need a place of my own and a job," she says.

He moves his toes away from hers. "No graduate school?"

She's said it. She can't take it back. "You're disappointed."

The bothersome muscle in his lower back aches from all the mopping. "Another image of you to give up." He presses his hand to his back and rubs. "Actually, I thought I wanted you to leave. You and Kate take over the house." He gives her foot a nudge, then reaches across the space between them to hug her.

126

If she wants a job, no typing drudgery, for God's sake. She laughs. A college graduate with a B.A. in English isn't exactly the hottest thing on the job market. He tells her to call Bob Hunt—he usually needs help at the gallery. Or Audrey. She's got plenty of business contacts. They stay close to each other, talking, while Kate watches from the attic window.

As she was sorting out things in the attic, Kate found her old dream notebooks on a forgotten shelf. They're piled in the chair. She turns from the window and studies her painting. Vibrant red, serious black, subtle orange. Grandfather Levinsky puts a hand on her shoulder and moves her to the notebooks. "Courage, sweetheart," he says.

The first drawing dates from the beginning of her work with Lonnie. A woman behind a fence. She has both hands against it, struggling to get out. Independence—Sheila wrote about that in her letter, about wanting to be free of Kate and Alex's ideas about her. When Kate made this drawing, she wanted out of her own depression and fear. She sinks to the floor next to the chair and goes through the notebook page by page. Five judges in heavy robes stare at her. A chaotic sky swirls, only one small, re-demptive, silver planet visible in it. She recognizes every drawing, but the tension is gone from them.

She's oddly happy. The house has been freed. The worst has happened. The intruders broke through more than a window. "I could give up the house now," she thinks, surprising herself. "What did I dream last night?"

Mac's photo of her is propped on her easel: She's in her rocking chair, just at the moment in the party when she saw Grandfather Levinsky appear between Alex and

127

Audrey on the couch. Kate is smiling, though she doesn't recall smiling and hadn't seen the smile in the tiny photo on the proof sheet. But it's her. All of it is her—the photo, the painting, the woman who sits on the attic floor discovering how so much fits together. The figure on the canvas isn't smiling, but with the photo close to it, it seems to.

She finds the dog that said, "Sacrifice guilt." The dream notebooks have served their purpose. Her work with Lonnie is long past. Her worries about Sheila are pointless. Sheila got through her life in San Francisco without Kate even knowing about the love spell, the disastrous affair with Hank, the turmoil.

Alex has gotten Kate through hard times. He worked with her this morning, mopping, putting things away. He told her that he's going to paint in the garage; he's given up running to Sam's. She reaches under her shirt to wipe away the sweat between her breasts. He didn't say much else, though, was preoccupied. Planning his first painting, she supposes. He gathered up the pieces of the shattered sibyl without even saying he was sorry it was broken. He knows what it meant to her. He paid for all that therapy.

Courage? It's never taken courage to love Alex. He's made it easy, but he's just not with her these days, and she's never talked to him about her red paintings or about getting old. The things that are really on her mind. Is it time for them to move aside for each other?

She goes to the window again. He's in the lawn chair. Sheila's gone. He leans over, elbows on his knees, chin in his hands, thinking. She can't see his face. His hair is pale in the hot sun. Alex is completely colorless in the thick afternoon light. He heaves himself out of the chair and walks to the garage with a heaviness she doesn't recognize. Is it even Alex?

The notebooks are bulky, but she gets them downstairs, grabs a box of matches on her way through the kitchen. There's an old metal trash bin behind the greenhouse. She pulls it to the middle of the yard, puts the notebooks in it, then lights match after match to set them on fire.

"Open fires are against the law," Alex says, coming out of the garage to see what she's doing. He leans over the bin, sees the black covers, resistant but doomed. They expand with the flames. The pages inside lift, then fall, then disintegrate. "Your dreams," he says.

The air fills with smoke. Kate feels the smoke in her nose, hears the rasp of dying pages. "Old ones," she says.

He's wanted something new for himself, but the break-in shook him. He owns this house, whatever he's said about not depending on property. It's his. He should make some decisions. Why didn't Kate ask him, for once, what he thought? She dragged out the trash bin, started the fire without saying a word. He stalks back to the garage and carries out the remains of an easel she used when she did her painting in the garage. As he throws the wooden pieces on the fire, he says, "Did you intend to burn the couch and piano, too, without asking me? How about our bed— shall we toss it on the fire?"

"They're my notebooks. That's my easel."

"Who bought the easel? Who set up the garage for you to work in?"

Smoke stings her eyes, her nose, gets onto her skin and into her hair. "Who the hell are you?" she shouts. She starts across the yard. Alex runs after her, brings her back to the trash bin.

"You started this," he says. "You can damn well watch it burn till it's finished." He holds onto her, his arms around her waist. They would look like lovers from a distance, but he says, "And who, dear Kate, are you? Have you ever let me read your dreams, see your notebooks, given me a single clue to what goes on inside your precious imagination?"

Sam Nakamura drives up to the house in his rickety pickup truck just in time for the end of the fire. "Hey!" he shouts. "Open fires—no good. Against the law."

"We're burning Kate's secrets," Alex says, letting go of her.

"The thieves didn't take those, huh?" Sam says.

Kate—angry, hot—says, "Okay, you two. You want to see my latest painting?"

"Yeah, if it's any good," Sam says.

She'll let Alex see what he wants to see—her imagination—her own face coming through on that canvas. He'll never be able to paint like that.

The three of them climb to the attic. Alex drops into the chair, shakes his head appreciatively. "It's good," he says.

Sam squints. "So, from the abstract to the mystical-realistic." He peers into the figure's face. "It's you, not you, more you than ever. Maybe Woman as Virgin—one with herself. You going to join the temple goddesses or go out in the street preaching inner strength as salvation, or what?" He steps back and plants his tough old arms across his chest. "Listen, that red likes itself the way it is. You

130

fool around with it, you mess it up. You sure about the black? Unmixed? Makes people look at it an awful lot. How come that orange is so cool? Earth after rain. I gave up on orange—too show-offy—but you know what you're doing." High praise from Sam. Kate gives Alex a quick, victorious look, but he's absorbed in her work and in listening to Sam.

"It's not too weird for buyers, either," Sam says. "They won't understand how you did this, but they'll understand how good it is. You going to find some buyers?" Kate shrugs. "You better," he says. "Get this out in the world. You owe the world something, even if you don't want to know it."

Kate brings out the three other canvases in the series. They talk about them, enthralled. "These are like your fire today," Sam says. "Getting rid of secrets." He smiles, his old tree bark face so ugly and so handsome that Kate smiles, too.

Sam says he came over to help—to see what damage was done during the break-in. Do they need him for anything?

"We're pretty much finished," Alex says. He gets up from the chair. "I want to buy paint and brushes at Sparrow's Art Supply—you want to come with me, Sam?"

"Nah. I know what art supplies look like."

Sheila has taken Alex's van to drive to Venice, to see a poet she knows out there. Can Alex borrow Kate's car? Sure. Sam and Alex leave. Kate lies down on the living room couch.

"You owe the world something," Sam said. Hasn't she done enough just by painting? She grabs a pillow from the foot of the couch and shoves it under her head. When she closes her eyes, Chagall's *The Flying Sleigh* comes to her. A golden sleigh, lifted by an enormous rooster. As she feels the pull of the sleigh above Russian roofs, she feels the pleasure of flying, but anxiety, too, at being taken away from what is familiar.

If Chagall had kept his work to himself, she wouldn't see these pictures in her mind, images she's carried for years. They first spoke to her of Alex—his Russian Jewish history, of Grandfather Levinsky, of a life not her own, a magical life. The life of art she's fought for and gained. The two shows at Bob's gallery have brought her at least a small reputation. "That's plenty," she's told herself. If she owes the world something, that means the world will look at her, comment and criticize. Galleries, museums, buyers, sellers. Other artists. The rooster pulls her higher. She's dizzy. "Courage, sweetheart." Grandfather Levinsky flies next to her.

Chagall's gold fades. Georgia O'Keeffe's painting of a stern black cross set against a fiery sky appears, burning Kate's eyes. The twenty-year-old Kate is dead. A forty-five-year-old Kate dies into the uncomfortable, hard pillow behind her head. She sacrifices her fantasy of growing orchids in the greenhouse, the comforts of a sheltered life.

8

AUDREY HEARS AN UNPLEASANT SOUND like a muffled power lawn mower. Her stomach hurts. She ought to get out of bed. It must be late. She opens her eyes on her bedroom: the cool beige walls, the cinnamon drapes. The beige rug is slightly darker than the walls. Three nineteenth century prints of wildflowers in shades of green, yellow, and brown hang on the wall next to the bed. Her own good taste. "And what did it get me?" she thinks. "A bellyache." Damn that scotch, and the chicken breasts, full of herbs and garlic.

Flower and Ming meow outside the closed bedroom door. She'll get up and feed them in a minute. Maybe she should see Dr. Hensely to be sure it's not her ulcer making her stomach sour and raw. She lifts herself on one elbow to check the clock on her dressing table. One o'clock. God, what will they think at the office? There is no office.

There's no one to think anything. Yesterday, that was a pleasure. Today, her lacy nightgown straps have slipped carelessly down her arms. She hitches them up roughly, as if they're responsible for something—for her sense that everything's slipping: her stomach out of control; her sleeping habits upset; her peace of mind lost in that sound she hears—what *is* that, anyway? Somebody's lawn mower. No, it's not that loud. She fishes under the bed for her slippers and plods to the door. The cats coo at her. They've won. She's up.

"Easy," she says to them. They crawl between her feet as she walks to the kitchen. In the hall next to her room, she passes a small table where her portable radio is playing. That's it—that's what she's heard—how did she forget it? Was it on last night while Kate was here? Must have been. She turns it up before she turns it off. A dramatic voice on the noncommercial FM station is reading from Lawrence Durrell's *Justine*: "The narrow street was of baked and scented terra cotta, soft now from rain but not wet. Its whole length was lined with the coloured booths of prostitutes whose thrilling marble bodies were posed modestly each before her doll's house, as before a shrine . . . the whole street was lit by a series of stabbing carbide-lamps standing upon the ground: throwing thirsty, ravishing violet shadows upwards into the nooks and gables of the dolls' houses, into the nostrils and eyes of its inhabitants, into the unresisting softness of that furry darkness. . . ." Audrey hasn't read this book, wouldn't recognize Durrell's name if she heard it. But she listens.

As she fell asleep last night, she imagined a man with her. She reached for him. She imagined that he reached

134

back. Her stomach churns. She's got to take some Mylanta before she does anything else. The cats stalk from the kitchen to the hall, the hall to the kitchen. "Easy," she says again.

As she gulps her dose of Mylanta, she catches sight of her face in the bathroom mirror. No, she doesn't want to look at herself yet.

Who was that man? Lush, black hair. Familiar, but nobody she knows. That old movie star, Tyrone Power. She adored his looks. Delicious shoulders. Oh, that's dumb. Fairy tales—little girls in boarding schools create imaginary men in their beds. Audrey hasn't indulged in that in years, doesn't want a '40s Robin Hood—no, that was Errol Flynn with his devilish face and muscular legs. She glances at the mirror. It reflects, behind her, the back of the bathroom door where her sea green satin robe hangs. "Why do I bother?" she asks herself, remembering the times she's put on the robe just to sit in the den and watch TV until bedtime. "It's for entertaining a man." She can't help but notice that the aloe vera cream didn't take away one wrinkle or even soften one.

The cats find her. Ming leaps onto the sink in front of her. Flower rubs at her legs. "Yes, yes," she says and goes to the kitchen. After she feeds them, she unlatches the cat door hinged at the bottom of the kitchen door. They slip out and head for the garden.

"How did the radio get on that station?" she wonders. FM stations slip occasionally. She had it tuned to the classical station, not the classical *classical* one, but the one that plays lighter music, pleasant to have in the background. She wanders back to the hall and turns on the radio again. The cultured, noncommercial voice is still with *Justine*: "Then the breathing and the sudden simultaneous playing of three pianos. . . . It was becoming harder and harder to pretend to be sane by the standards of ordinary behaviour. . . ." The nightgown straps creep down her arms. She flips off the radio and goes back to her bedroom. All that talk with Kate about men! She sits on the bed, reaches under her nightgown to her pubic hair and under that to the soft lips of her vagina. She reaches as she imagined the man reaching into her last night. She pulls her hand away. "Boarding school," she growls. The humiliation of—at her age—the foolishness of—is she going to wake up every morning from now on masturbating?

The man in her bed last night moves on top of her and says, "Let me love you." She finds her vagina again, surrenders to the warmth there—that strong, sexual juice—and she lies back on the bed, moving in herself until the man whispers, "Oh, yes, oh, yes, oh, yes," and she shudders with her own orgasm. It's the first she's had in at least—since Carl from Seattle used to come into town. That long? She puts her hand to her nose, smells her body, can't imagine that she's doing this—smelling herself, smelling the way she and Roy used to—but that was half a lifetime ago. Forget Roy. Forget Tyrone Power. It's time to take some classes, entertain friends at witty dinner parties. It's time to—

To what? She sits up. "I'd like to fuck a regiment," she says to the beige walls.

The sourness in her stomach has eased. She's hungry. Soft-boiled eggs. "Like a patient in a hospital," she thinks, disgusted with the idea of soft-boiled anything. Well, she's got to eat. Should she cook here or go down to the restaurant on Hillhurst where they have such nice lunches? She could sit outside on the patio there, unless it's another scorcher. The air conditioning has been on "Low" all night, so it's cool in the house. She'd better take a stroll around the garden, check on the roses and their aphid population, see what the weather is like. What will she do after lunch? "Shopping," but there's nothing she needs. "A movie." Movies in the afternoon are something you do when you're depressed. "Call Flo." Maybe. "I could drop by and see Kate and Alex." Maybe. Make an appointment with Dr. Hensely. "I'm not sick!" she shouts to the garden as she steps out the back door, still in her nightgown.

The Mr. Lincoln roses, smooth and velvety, offer themselves to her. The blooms sway at the tops of their stems—perfect cups of red. She leans into them. "You're wonderful," she says, wishing she could find rose perfume like that, but no rose perfume—and she's sniffed hundreds of them—ever smelled like real roses to her. The flowers of the whole garden shine: her proud roses, the bushes she's planted diligently over the years. Thirty bushes, every single one with its own history. "You Angel Faces," she says, turning to the lavender blossoms, "from that nursery way out in the West Valley." She moves over to the Honor roses, white as Kate's face as a child. "Suicide?" she thinks. Kate's confession disturbed her. The Honors have complex blooms, ruffled and multi-petaled. She tries to catch their elusive scent. She'd like to take some in the house but can't bear to cut any today. Funny, that usually doesn't bother her.

"Let them live," she says to Ming, who's rolling in the

137

dirt under the bush. "Let the floribundas and the gran-
difloras and the hybrid teas all live today." She bends to
give Ming a pat on his upturned belly and notices the stem
of the bush. Aphids. Pale green, squishy things. She's tried
Sevin and Pyrethrum and Diazinon and Cygon. A losing
battle. Her beautiful roses—all the beauty she ever wanted,
here in her own yard, gathered by her hard work, by
searching out those peculiar nurseries—and now the magic
is being ruined by aphids. "I'll get you yet," she promises,
lifting her nightgown to step through the row of bushes
toward the garden hose.

"I can't water now," she remembers. "Too hot. I'll
have to wait until evening." She wants at least to wash
off the aphids until she can get some new advice about
what to kill them with. Water at this time of day steams
things up, doesn't do the roses any good. She could scream.
The Queen Elizabeths are lovely—look at that pink, like
the inside of Ming's ears—so delicate—and look at the
leaves, all gooey with aphids. Audrey stomps back to the
house, taking off her bedroom slippers in the kitchen.
"Shouldn't have worn them out in the yard," she mutters,
looking at how much dirt the soft cloth soles have picked
up. "I'll have to put them in the washer, and I just washed
them."

She can't bear to waste soap and water, time, her life.
Has she? Kate said no, but what does Kate know? Yet
Kate was so loving last night. Kate knows plenty, Audrey
supposes. Oh, those stories about Sheila going through a
young woman crisis—men and writing and money and
independence and love. Dear God. And Alex wanting to
paint, worrying Kate. Not what Audrey wanted to hear.

"I'll die if Kate and Alex split up." What a thought. She heads for the refrigerator for a glass of milk. She can't imagine Kate and Alex apart, even if she's never wanted them together. Sheila's face appears, an opaque overlay on Kate's childhood face. Girlhood and white roses.

The day Sheila was born, Audrey couldn't leave her office. The new fall line was being modeled; she had to see it—it was her only chance to inspect the whole line at once. She wasn't a vice-president yet, just one of those assistants to a vice-president, but she had to know what was being designed and produced. Alex called, excited, had to wait five minutes on the other end of the phone while somebody found Audrey. "Marvelous!" she said, although she didn't have time to ask what they'd named the baby, only found out that it was an eight pound girl. She'd dashed back to the showroom, afraid she'd missed something important.

She had. She'd missed seeing Kate in the hospital, nursing Sheila for the first time. She'd missed the look on Alex's face when he brought Kate and Sheila home: awe and pleasure and nervousness so tender that Kate burst into tears, seeing him, and he'd had to carry Sheila into the apartment.

When Audrey got around to visiting, Sheila was a week old. She began to have her own face early, was more than newborn by the time Audrey got a glimpse of her fuzzy, fierce hair. "Whose hair is that?" she'd asked. "The priest I slept with," Kate said, disgusted.

Audrey decides she'll go to the store and buy groceries. It's too hot for the patio at the restaurant. The milk has satisfied her for now. She'll cook a nice dinner later.

By the time she's through shopping at Weston's, though, she's starving. She parks the two bags of groceries on her kitchen counter, pours herself another glass of milk, and paws through the bags to find the peaches and cottage cheese. "I probably shouldn't eat peaches—the rough skin and acid." But the peaches tempt her. She can count on Weston's to have the best. She washes and peels and slices a fat peach, arranges it in a dish, scoops cottage cheese onto it, gets a fork, and eats ravenously as she stands at the counter. Peering into her grocery bags, she thinks, "I bought enough for an army." She eyes the prime rib. It was expensive, but she'll have great leftovers. Four o'clock. If she gets it in the oven now, it'll be ready by five-thirty or six, at the latest.

The doorbell chimes its two melodious notes. She's not expecting anyone, peeks out the peephole to see who it is. Sheila, who's about to ring the bell again. As Audrey opens the door, Sheila nearly knocks her over with a hug. "I've got a job! Invite me to dinner!"

"You're invited," Audrey says, catching her breath. Sheila's so excited that she's getting ready to hug her again. Audrey retreats and asks, "What kind of a job?"

Sheila, a baby, her little face in the crib surrounded by wild hair. Audrey didn't even pick her up the first time she saw her because Kate had made that dreadful remark about the priest. She'd huffed out of the apartment, then had to make up with Kate over the phone from the office the next day, trying to apologize and write press releases at the same time. She did want to know her granddaughter. "I do love the baby," she'd whispered into the phone. Then someone came in with an urgent request from the

May Company junior department about their back-to-school promotion, and she'd had to hang up.

Sheila, that baby, tall now, like Alex, with something of Kate in her cheekbones and high forehead. Even in her excitement, she isn't one of those giggly young things Audrey sees all too often in this city. Sheila has firm legs, healthy arms. The old farm family echoes, which touches Audrey, even as she notices the foreign skin—too swarthy for a Kansas farm girl.

"I'm not starting at the top, that's for sure," Sheila says, circling the room. Audrey, avoiding another ferocious hug, sits on the couch. "What kind of a job?" she asks again.

"I went to see this poet Livia, and she said there were maybe jobs—apprenticeships—at a literary foundation out in Venice. They've got a library, and they publish a magazine of L.A. writing every month. They get grants and donations. Right now, they can hire a couple of people for a year to learn about putting the magazine together, sorting out the library—things like that. Livia took me to meet the woman in charge—Evie—and Evie talked to me, asked about San Francisco State, then went off to consult with somebody else, came back, and said that if I didn't mind working for peanuts, they'd let me start at the first of next week! There are always writers hanging out there, and they have readings—oh, Audrey, I've got a job in literature!"

"For one year. Earning peanuts. Forty hours a week?"

"About twenty-five. I'll have time to write."

"What's this place called?"

"The Laboratory."

141

"Sounds like experiments on helpless animals."

"The name is about alchemy. Transforming people's creative efforts into gold—you know, new visions, different forms of writing that haven't been tried before—aiming toward—"

"Who's this Livia?"

"A friend."

Sheila sinks onto the couch next to Audrey. What a day. What a beautiful day. She knew, the minute she met Livia at her apartment, that she'd done the right thing by calling her and driving out to Venice to meet her. Livia made tea, chatted about the beach being too crowded in the summer, waited for Sheila to get comfortable, then asked about her writing. Sheila stuttered for a few minutes, then loosened up, had more tea, talked about feeling educated but stupid.

Livia pulled out a poem she'd been working on and showed it to Sheila. It was good—every line was strong. "How long have you been writing?" Sheila had asked. Livia told her about the years she's spent trying to write magazine articles for money, but a lyrical voice always crept in. Too strange for editors. "So," she laughed, "I decided to pay attention to that funny thing that kept sneaking into my writing. Turns out it was poetry."

"I don't know what I want to write," Sheila admitted.

"It takes awhile. Just write and see what wants to write you."

Just write and get a job and get a place and—

For now, it's easy. Sheila has had one of those rare days on which everything seems to have been prepared ahead of time. It was all waiting for her. Livia. The job. And

Sheila will find a place where she can live alone—barely room for a bed and chair and desk, but she'll find it. When she is Kate's age, when she is Audrey's age, she'll think of the small apartment as vibrant, full of light. One of Kate's red paintings will hang on the wall: three figures all really one figure.

After Sheila divorces her first husband, she'll take her child, a boy who looks like Grandfather Levinsky, and live with Livia for a few months, will visit Kate often so that Kate can dote on the boy, sketch him endlessly. On one of those sad, recuperative days, they'll get the news that Audrey is dead at seventy-six from cancer of the stomach. Sheila will cry at Audrey's grave, never knowing the re-mark Audrey made about her baby hair, only knowing that Audrey bought her a bicycle on a special birthday. Freedom. Sheila will cry over losing the bike when Alex cleans out the garage this very afternoon. He asks her, as she heads for Venice, if she wants it, and she says, "No, I'm through with it." She's through with it for today, forever, although she'll stand crying into the multitude of roses that Audrey's friends will send to the grave site, wishing for the bike.

She'll have another husband and child but will still think back to her first light-filled apartment and want that, too. The pleasure of living alone, eating and writing when she felt like it. She will grieve for Audrey long after everyone else has stopped. Audrey, the grandmother who, as far as Sheila can see, doesn't need as much family as other people do, who has a house to herself, who has, in spite of her quirks, always represented to Sheila a solid, independent life without complications.

"Did you like it when Kate left home?" Sheila asks.

"Kate left to marry your father. No, I didn't like it. But I like it now." She does, she realizes. "I want to get the prime rib in the oven. Come on out in the kitchen and we'll talk. Do you get to wear nice clothes for this job, or is it one of those jeans and ugly shoe places?"

"Jeans—old ones. Running shoes. Everybody jogs at the beach, I guess."

Ming and Flower come in from the garden to greet Sheila. "Meow," Sheila says to them, lifting Flower to hold on her lap as she sits on a tall kitchen stool, watching Audrey salt and pepper the meat. She's getting tired, remembers that she's menstruating. She's glad to sit and hold the cat close to her.

"Do Kate and Alex know about this job?"

"I haven't been home yet." Sheila attends to a leaf that's caught in Flower's fur. "I wanted to come here first. I thought you'd understand—about jobs and things. You know."

Audrey feels tears rise to her eyes. "Don't," she tells herself. "Be dignified." But it hasn't been a very dignified day, all around. She lets the tears come. The Rock. But with the loss of her vice-presidency, there just isn't anything to sell anymore. She has eleven years left to listen to Sheila, to Sheila's first child, who will delight Audrey with his curious, wise, old man's face. With more grace than anger, more relief than regret, she will listen to her own life fading. And, more presently, she'll find time, tomorrow, to listen to John Elliott from the Shakespearean two-story across the street. He'll appear in her garden with a new cure for aphids. Realizing that the neighborhood is infested with them this summer, he'll assume that Audrey will want to know about the homemade mixture he's concocted—experimented with until it really works on those bugs. She'll certainly listen to that. Then, she'll listen to John's story of his loneliness since his wife died a year ago, and to his special recipe for martinis.

So Audrey cries to herself, which helps her listen, and Sheila tells her all over again about the job, Livia, Venice and the ocean and poetry.

Finally, Audrey says, "Shall we invite Kate and Alex to dinner?"

"Alex—yeah, he'd like that. Kate? I'm not sure. I don't know what she's thinking about me."

"She loves you."

Sheila picks at Flower's fur, although there aren't any more leaves to dislodge. "How do you know?"

"She said so. We had a long talk last night."

"Before the break-in?"

Audrey turns. "What break-in?"

"Oh, God, hasn't anybody told you about that?"

Kate heard the phone ring about four-thirty but was out in the garage watching Alex string up a wobbly row of electric light bulbs. Couldn't he think of anything more professional, more painterly, than this dangling bunch of bulbs over his easel?

"I've got enough paint to last me a year. I may never leave this garage. You'll have to bring me trays of food and apologize to our friends."

Kate retreated to the house, where, as night comes, she

145

sits in the living room with the front door open, letting the odor of star jasmine find her.

"Shall we sell the house?" she asked Alex this afternoon. He looked at her as if she'd kicked him, hard. The dream notebooks are ashes, cold in the metal trash bin. Kate settles back in the rocking chair and drifts.

Sheila's surprised to find the door open. She thought Kate and Alex had gone out when she and Audrey couldn't get them on the phone. "Kate?" Of course it's Kate, but the woman in the rocking chair, sitting under one dim lamp, looks older than Kate. Sheila kneels on the floor with her back to her mother. "Rub my neck, would you?" Kate does. "Just what I need," Sheila says. As Kate massages, Sheila talks—about her job, then about Audrey, who's outraged that they didn't have bars on all their windows and a burglar alarm for the house. Then she says, "I'm going to Venice tomorrow to look for an apartment."

"You'll need money." Kate moves her hands to Sheila's shoulders.

Sheila closes her eyes and lets go of a hard knot in one muscle. "Right."

"The money from the painting is still yours. Do anything you like with it."

"I'll pay it back."

Kate moves to sit next to Sheila, feels the old hardwood floor under her. "You don't have to. Let's not owe each other what we don't owe. You don't owe me what I want to give you."

"Did Alex tell you that I'm through with Mac—and Ralph?"

"No."

"I love Ralph. I just can't be with him."

146

"How does that feel?"

"Is it possible to laugh and cry at the same time?"

They sit, not talking, thinking together in the middle of the city that moves around them, is benignly indifferent as the moon shifts from Scorpio to Sagittarius, a gentler influence. The three thieves decide, cruising in their car a mile away, that there's nothing more they can steal from Kate and Alex and Sheila. In fact, maybe they'd better cool it for now. The cops stopped Creeper for running a red light and got suspicious, like they knew something, like maybe they were putting something together about the robberies.

Sheila goes to the piano. She plays the Bach exercises, the music she threw in the trash. She's memorized that music in herself, in a place that she didn't want to remember yesterday. Listening, Kate thinks of Alex. How would she paint him, if she could, tonight? "He'd be sitting out in the yard in an old chair. I'd paint him from the attic window the way I saw him today, not able to really see anything." She likes the image of a chair with a distant figure seen from above, but it saddens her. It's taken the place of intimate hands and hair, of the owl with its reassuring aphorisms.

Alex wanders in, too tired to paint anymore. He eases onto the couch, closes his eyes, and listens to the music. Kate has closed her eyes, too, and doesn't open them.

Sheila plays all the Bach exercises, then Bartók pieces for children, exquisitely dissonant. Kate opens her eyes. In the dim light, Alex looks as far away as he looked in the yard. The playing stops. Sheila says, "Hi, Alex. Where were you?"

"Painting in the garage." He supposes that's what to

147

call it. The paint didn't move the way he wanted it to. "Have you got any grass?" The goddamn thieves took his stash.

"I've got a joint that Ralph gave me yesterday. It's upstairs. Sinsemilla—it will get you off if anything will."

"You don't want it?"

"No." Ralph. The motel. She goes upstairs.

"Come on," Alex says to Kate.

Kate locks the door, turns off the lamp, and, in the dark, they climb the stairs. He puts his arm around her. She can't tell if he's steadying himself or truly wants to touch her.

"Have a good time," Sheila says, coming to the door of her bedroom with the joint. Alex's hand is stained with paint. Her father, vulnerable, wanting a joint enough to ask her for it. They all say good night, the "Good nights" echoing through the hall. Sheila's never believed that Kate and Alex would get old. Alex's hair is getting so gray. Kate's shoulders are thin. She wants to call after them, but all she says is "Good night" one last time as they close the door to their room.

Kate undresses and falls into bed, asleep before Alex can offer her the joint. He sits on the bed, smoking, feeling the rush of sinsemilla in his head and the roughness of dry paint on his hands. It should thrill him. It doesn't. He rubs his fingers. "Why did Kate think of selling the house? No reason to. No reason not to. No reason for us to be together. Or apart. All that paint all over the damn canvas. There's got to be some reason." His thinking circles, goes nowhere. He smokes, then undresses. Slips into bed. Rubs his hand over Kate's ass. She rolls away from him. He kisses the back of her neck, and when she turns to him, she runs her hand down his belly to his penis, finds him erect. She brushes the coarse hair on his thigh. Bristly hair, not Alex's gentleness. She moves her hand back to his belly but finds the same hair. Alex, kissing her breasts, finds the hollow between them. His mouth is buried in something that isn't soft at all, is solid bone.

They lie together, then Alex moves off of her, says, "I'm sorry."

"Forgiveness comes at the end of something," she mumbles.

"Can't we stop saying that?" He pulls the sheet over himself.

"Let me have some of the sheet."

Neither of them can imagine being in another house, yet what Kate sees as she falls asleep again is an apartment like the one Sheila will rent tomorrow: a place just large enough for a woman to live in alone, to sit at a desk and stare out of the window toward the ocean, smelling salt and her own body.

9

KATE, ON WEDNESDAY, meanders through the house, sipping coffee before she starts to paint. It will be cool today, autumnal in the middle of summer. She sips, steps onto the front porch to enjoy the fresh morning air. Above the hills, real sky. There won't be much smog. Los Angeles: vicious heat and choking smog, then relief. Seasons within seasons. Not the simple God of Kate's Midwestern childhood, but many gods. Anything can happen. A fine morning to paint, to look into the woman's face on her canvas and discover even more about herself, about change. When Audrey pulls up in her white Cadillac, Kate waves enthusiastically. "You got up early," she says as Audrey hurries up the steps to the porch.

"Too early. I've gotten to be a real stay-abed." Audrey throws her arms around Kate, splashing coffee on herself. "Sheila said you were all right, but I had to be sure—those thieves, the house—"

Theft. Pain. Relief. The power of Los Angeles is in its abundance of moods, its multiple gods. Audrey rubs at the dribble of coffee on her crisp dress. Oh, forget the dress. She appraises her daughter. Good color in her face. Clear eyes. Healthy, slender, smiling. "You're really all right?"

"Sure." Kate turns to Audrey. Audrey's face, even in a few days, has softened. The vice-president is barely visible. Kate sees a handsome, sensual woman, a woman who is learning to sleep late. Anything can happen.

A mile away, on Vermont Avenue, the older woman Kate imagined on Sunday behind the door of her apartment, wanting to swim, emerges from that door, ready for shopping. A cool morning. She'll pick up the shampoo she needs, cigarettes, Kleenex. She tucks her purse under her arm as she walks south toward Barnsdall Shopping Center with its Woolworth's and Thrifty Drug and See's Candy and other small shops lining the side of the hill that leads up to Barnsdall Park.

The park lifts above the neighborhood. It holds an art museum, a Frank Lloyd Wright house, a children's art center, all shaded by olive trees. The woman thinks she might go up there to relax after she does her shopping. At the bus stop in front of Rocco's, the Italian restaurant and bakery, the young woman who's always stoned is wandering the street with her jeans unzipped and her belly showing. She holds a bit of flower to her forehead. The older woman avoids her, avoids the possibility that the young one might speak to ask for the time or small change or a home. "Nobody loves her," the woman thinks, but she doesn't know. No one knows, just as no one knows the whole history of this city or what will happen next.

The older woman pauses at the stoplight on the corner

151

of Vermont and Hollywood Boulevard. She watches the buzzing traffic cautiously as she waits for the light to change. Does someone run up behind her and snatch her purse? Or does she step off the curb a moment too soon and find herself tangled in the wheels of a motorcycle? Does the frightened motorcyclist, shuffling his helmet from hand to hand, say to the police and onlookers, "Hey, I just didn't see her, you know?" Or does she cross the street, do her shopping, feel pleased with the shampoo that advertises a perfect pH balance for her hair, then take her walk in the park, enjoying the city below her, stretching around the hill? Does she promise herself to definitely take a swim this afternoon, no matter who's out there by the pool, no matter how heavy her thighs are?

Kate, getting ready to go to the attic, finds a smock in the closet that she bought once to wear when she paints, a cotton thing printed with jungle flowers in fanciful purple and yellow. She bought it in a fit of pleasure but has never worn it. It's frivolous compared with Alex's old shirts. She puts it on, admiring the audacity of the artist who designed this fabric—these bursting, obtrusive flowers that have never existed except in the imagination of Los Angeles.

Who here can name all the gods? In the park, the older woman sees a shape tremble between the olive trees, just for a second. A man? An animal? Maybe it's Pan, dead for two thousand years. Maybe Pan has found life again on a hill in Los Angeles.

Grandfather Levinsky's ghost, watching his great-granddaughter as she drives toward Venice to rent an apartment, prays the traditional Jewish morning prayer,

152

"My God, the soul which Thou has given me is pure." Sheila hears the prayer, not in words but in her feeling of being free for today, pure for today, of being simply who she is.

Kate studies her painting. So much is ending for her, yet here's the beginning of her best work. The series of paintings began early this year. The yearning figures do yearn toward something. They move to what the decade ahead will bring. Audrey's death. Sam's death. Kate's entrance into her fifties. Sheila's fertile years. It is all turning; it can't stop turning. Kate mixes the potent red that she wants to add to her painting.

At the Italian restaurant, the brioches bake steadily in the huge oven behind the restaurant. At Grand Central Market downtown, Asian and Latino stallkeepers stack green beans and exotic spices and fresh fish. In Venice, roller skaters, street musicians, zanies and tourists crowd the boardwalk. Jizo, the deity who stands on the lower level of the Ahmanson Gallery at the Los Angeles County Museum of Art, still stands, waiting for anyone who needs a little compassion.

At the apartment Sheila's going to find, the landlady is cleaning the stove. She complains to her husband about the messiness of the last tenant. "I hope we get somebody nice this time," she says, sliding her arm across her forehead. "Get me a bandanna, will you, Jack?" she asks, sending her husband off for a scarf to keep the sweat from dripping into her eyes. It's hard work, putting a place in order after someone has moved out. It's hard work ordering the fragments of Los Angeles, but the gods assist.

"Not bad last night," Ralph thinks as he wakes up at

153

home, coming out of sleep with music in his head. The stuff the group played at the Cuba Club got a lot of applause. A manager kind of guy talked to Danny afterward, said a club in West L.A. might hire them. Ralph shoves himself out of bed and grabs for his pants. He's gonna call Danny right now, find out what that guy had to say. The money from last night's gig is on the dresser. Cash. Enough to keep him out of his brother's auto shop for a couple of weeks. He smiles at the money, then at his mother who's coming in to see if her lazy son is up yet—almost afternoon. She smiles back at him, tells him that her homemade tortillas are still warm on the back of the stove. If he wants eggs, she's got time to cook because Linda, Louie's girl, offered to take the laundry and do it with hers at the Launderland. "Are they ever going to get married?" she asks Ralph. He puts his arm around his mother, whispers, "Tell her to get pregnant, then he'll marry her," which makes his mother laugh and slap at him at the same time.

Ralph remembers Sheila, lovely, naked. Too bad. A dead end. He says his secret soul name to himself, a prayer, the name a coyote gave him long ago in the mountains, the name that entered Ralph through peyote, through the stars, through the names of old Aztec gods. That name will always be his.

Audrey, at Weston's Market, hopes to find the perfect ham for tomorrow night. Kate has promised that she and Alex and Sheila will come for dinner. Audrey peers at the various pink packages, thinking of how many hams she's cooked in her life. But this is the present ham, the important one, the one still to be baked, glazed, eaten. "Let me choose the best," she says to the God of Food, whom she prays is listening.

154

Kate's painting is nearly finished. This is it. The final one in the series, the end of this absorbing exploration. The face on the canvas, hers and not hers, needs just a bit more here and there. She steps to the attic window for a moment, feeling the painting move out of her. "I'm coming," she says to the city as she picks up a fresh brush.

Kate paints into the afternoon, forgetting everything except the way the brush moves, steady in her hand, as if it's being held by someone else. She stands back to look at what she's done and hears the phone. She catches it in the upstairs hall before it stops ringing.

"Hi, Kate."

Bob Hunt.

"Kate?"

"Hi, Bob."

"Is Alex around?"

"Alex?"

"Your husband, remember?"

Kate breathes. "He's at work. At the committee."

"Oh, right—the educational thing. When does that end?"

"Late August."

"Look, I hate to push, but I just got a call from Gill Institute. They're in a hurry to find a part-time painting teacher for September. Somebody canceled on them. I want to suggest Alex. He's taught there before. I don't know why they threw this in my lap. I'm on the advisory board, but this isn't really my job. They're desperate, so I said okay, okay, I'll see what I can do. I thought I'd better get Alex on the phone and check it out with him."

Kate holds the paintbrush in the steady hand that's finishing her best work yet. "I'll teach at Gill," she says.

155

"You're kidding. You've never wanted to do any of that—you always said you had to concentrate on your own work. You've looked down your nose at painters who taught—come on, you have—even at Alex."

"I apologize to all the painters in the world who teach, all right?" She wonders why on earth she does want to teach at Gill when she has no idea what teaching means, only knows that she hates to talk in public. She will have to talk, won't she? She can't stand there in front of the students without saying anything. She imagines herself lecturing, demonstrating, with an eager group of young people listening. She wants to teach. "I don't have to have some kind of teaching credential, do I?"

"No, you've got enough education. You just have to be a good painter and a good teacher."

He's irritated, thinks she's acting smart. "What's a good teacher?" she asks, seriously.

"Look, maybe I should talk to Alex. I love you, Kate. I think you're the best of the best when it comes to painting and in certain other ways, too, which we won't talk about since we've decided not to—but—hold on, somebody just walked into the office."

Kate waits. Sam taught art by direct confrontation. She'd be kinder. Honest but encouraging. Sam was harsh. Still, his approach did work. What is a good teacher?

"Kate? I'm back. Listen, why do you want to do this?"

"Because I owe something to the world."

That stops him. Finally, he says, "It's not easy, helping kids get to their art."

"How much do I have to talk?"

"You've never taught anything before! Who knows whether Gill is even going to take a chance on you?"

156

"I'm a graduate of Gill. I'm an artist. I've had shows. I work all the time. I know as much about painting as anybody at Gill."

"Is this my Kate who inhabits the farthest corner of the room at openings of her own shows?"

"Just exactly how much do I have to talk?"

"You have to make speeches on every aspect of painting. You have to lecture and lead discussions, have individual conferences with students, make presentations before the administrative board about your course of study. You have to talk constantly, uninterruptedly."

"Sam never did." Kate keeps her grip on the paintbrush. "Do I have to meet someone at Gill? Do they have to take a look at me before I start teaching?"

Silence. Then, "I'll have to call them. They'll certainly want to interview you." Then a silence so long that she wonders if he's still on the line. "You may not get the job. I don't know who else they're talking to."

"I want it."

"Because you owe something to the world. Right. But is this what you owe? It's hard work. It's not natural work for you, Katie. You might fail miserably, and then you'd hate me for suggesting it."

"You didn't suggest it. I did. I'll never hate you."

"How will Alex feel?"

"I don't know. We'll see."

"I'll call you within the next couple of days."

"Great. Thanks for—" But he's off the phone.

Back in the attic, she studies her painting, a palimpsest of its own history now. It's so personal that she can't imagine how she missed seeing herself in it for so long. It's taken on all of its impersonal history, too. She un-

157

derstands that. How could she talk to students about this mixture of actual life and imagination, about the physical work—the skill—but also the creative mystery of art?

She starts downstairs, finished with her work for the day. There's frantic knocking at the front door. She hurries. Alex? He'd let himself in. Mac's voice. He shouts, "Sheila? Sheila!" When Kate opens the door, he throws himself on her before he realizes that she isn't Sheila. He groans, untangles himself. "I've got to see Sheila, give her one more chance, ask her to come with me. I'm leaving tomorrow on that filming assignment—I got it—I'm going to Nevada to shoot film of wild horses. We can get married in Vegas—have a honeymoon—we can—" He's wearing his "Casablanca" T-shirt. Valiant souls will win out.

"Sheila's not here. She's out looking for an apartment."

"An apartment?" She hasn't been thinking about him at all. She's gone off to find a place to live by herself. He bangs angrily at the side of the door. He pounds to get Sheila to listen, even though she isn't in the house. He's sure she must love him if he loves her.

Kate's afraid Mac will hurt his hands. "Come on. Now, don't—" She pulls at him.

Alex, home from the committee, runs onto the porch. He manages to hold onto Mac, whose anger finally shoves itself out in one final, massive grunt. He relaxes into Alex's arms. "Come in the house," Alex says.

There's not much to say when the three of them are settled around the oak table and Kate has given Mac a cold beer. He drinks in gulps, apologizes, rubs his stinging fists.

"Well, anyway, congratulations on the job," Alex says.

Kate brings a dish of peanuts. Mac concentrates on

158

shelling them while he tells Kate and Alex how much he loves Sheila. Do they think she's forgotten him so soon—two years together is a pretty long time for a couple of people to love each other—could she forget him just like that?

"Not just like that," Alex says.

After a few minutes, they leave him at the table, tell him to take it easy, stay for a while. Alex makes his way to the garage to get more paint on his canvas. Kate goes out to buy food for dinner. "Crab salad," she decides. "Help yourself to another beer," she calls to Mac as she closes the back door behind her.

He sits, focusing on the peanuts. He decides to shell every one of them. Hunching over the dish, he tries to keep the shells and nutmeats separate. If he can do it, keep his mind on the nuts and shells, do a good job of it, maybe something will happen. What? Something. If he can get these things in neat piles, maybe—

Sheila drives up to the house, full of the airy apartment she's found, available right this minute. She's paid the first month's rent, the last month's rent, a cleaning fee. The receipt and a key are in her jeans pocket.

Mac's car. She was going to write him a letter, meant to do it last night, but what could she say that she didn't say when she told him no on the porch? No. She walks into the house without anything else to offer. She can't see what Mac is doing at the table, but he looks like a priest in an old-fashioned novel, counting rosary beads, praying intensely. Where did their plans go so fast? His apartment, his bed, the times they've spent holding each other, talking about grad school, his work, marriage. It's as if those plans never existed, as if Mac and Sheila never

159

made love or sat on the bed sharing a pizza, planning. The memories belong to somebody else.

She called Livia again today. They made plans. Nothing big—not like Mac's idea of marriage and a whole life together. Just plans to meet at a poetry reading on Friday night. Livia will introduce Sheila to other writers. That's the only kind of plan she wants. Mac's counting peanuts, she realizes, as she moves into the kitchen.

"Hi," she says, slipping into a chair across the table from him.

"Oh, God." He jumps up and reaches for her, but she stands up.

"Don't," she says. "Let's just talk for a while."

He sits down as she paces the kitchen, picking a sprig of parsley from Kate's window box, nibbling it as Mac tells her about his job, about getting married in Las Vegas, about loving her.

The parsley tastes peppery, earthy. The rent receipt in her pocket feels real, more real than any talk about love. She goes to the window box again, chews on another bit of parsley, stares out into hills that are settling in the afternoon light. She says, "I found a place today. I'm moving in as soon as I can. I'm going to write. I've got a job, too—that starts next week. Hey, I'm sorry. I'm really, really sorry, but it was never what I wanted—marriage and all that—I should have known, but I swear I didn't— I swear I thought we could—but we can't. You need somebody who—" She wants to describe a perfect woman for Mac, but she knows he thinks she's the perfect one. "It won't ever work," she tells him.

He stands behind her and puts his arms around her. She can't bear having him so close, but she can't move.

He lays his face against her neck. "Where's your place?" he whispers, brushing his mouth on her skin.

"In Venice."

"Real funky and bohemian, huh?" He stops nuzzling her. There's an edge in his voice.

"I hadn't thought of it like that. It's close to the ocean and my job. I like it out there." It is bohemian, she knows, but what a fusty old word. She would have said "artistic," "risky," "just what I need."

Then, it's over. They both feel it. Mac loosens his grip. Sheila sits down. There's nothing left in either of them for each other, although Mac will cry on the plane, flying to Nevada, and Sheila will cry, in a week, when she's settled in her apartment and is unpacking the final box of books. She'll pick up one that Mac gave her for Christmas last year: a collection of Gertrude Stein's lectures and essays. He tried. He certainly tried.

"I've always liked that T-shirt," she says. He rubs at the rubbery, romantic faces of Bogart and Bergman on his chest. His odd piles of nuts and shells are still in the dish.

He gives her a wry smile. "I'm just as crazy as anybody," he says.

She hears the front door close so quietly that she almost doesn't hear it, but when she does, she goes to the door. Mac is getting into his car. "I could write a lot about endings," she thinks, knowing what Kate knows: It's the last summer of a large part of their lives. Kate lets the back door slam as she comes in from her trip to the seafood shop. Sheila turns to the kitchen to help her with dinner.

Although it's not dark outside yet, Alex has the lights on in the garage. The electric bulbs make lines and colors

161

too stark, but he can't see to paint without them. He coaxes his brush across the canvas, squinting as the string of lights wobbles above him.

He'll never make this painting come alive. It won't surrender to him. He will understand this only when he has another dream, one that will take him out of the garage forever.

Kate brings a tray for him—crab salad, a glass of white wine. Pushing aside his tubes of paint, she settles the tray on a low wooden table near Alex's easel. Then she takes a look at his canvas.

"Why does it promise so much and give so little?" he asks.

"Scared?"

"I *want* to do this."

All her old paraphernalia is gone from the garage, discarded with the easel that Alex burned yesterday. He's pasted photos on the back wall—Rauschenberg's "combines," collections of found objects, the junk of life transformed into art. Alex had a passion for those things in the '50s. It isn't the '50s. "He's not making it work," Kate thinks. "He's mixed decent colors—those blues and grays are interesting, but they aren't holding. All the nonsense about time for himself. All the drama of going to Sam's. All that foolishness about being left out. If he wants something of his own, he's not going to get it by painting." She can't bear the sight of the sloppy paint barely hanging on the canvas. "I'll have to bear it. If I want to teach, I'll have to put up with a lot worse canvases than this, and be patient, not blow up in people's faces." But Alex? He should know better. "Well, he doesn't." She watches his nervous hand, the shaking brush, with a rush of love. She will bear it, she promises herself, if she has to, with as much patience as he's had for her work.

"You took me seriously about bringing trays out here," Alex says, putting the brush aside. He sits cross-legged on the floor. "Have a chair," he says, gesturing to the cement.

"Bob Hunt called today. There's a teaching job at Gill this fall."

"Somebody else can have it. I'm fed up with jobs in education."

"I'd like to make a change myself, this fall."

He flings his fork into his salad plate. "And do what? Divorce me? Sell the house? Fed up, Kate?"

The garage with its harsh light bulbs, the wretched canvas—she doesn't want to fight, doesn't want any of this picking they've learned to do without ever intending to learn it—pouting and sulking and not even making love happily. "Let's end this summer. Let's say it's over right now."

The silence between them is the silence of the night when Sheila was ten, when Kate tried to tear up the sketches of the child they both loved. And the silence at the end of Kate's white paintings when Alex walked into the garage and said, "Windows," admitting that he knew more than he—or Kate—thought he did about what she'd been suffering.

Alex looks into her face, the moon white beauty of her. "So," he says, retrieving his fork, "what's the new thing you want to do?"

"I want the job at Gill. Bob said he'd see if they'd consider me."

"Terrific!" He grins at her.

"You think so?"

"Terrific!" Alex used to stand around the coffee machine at Gill hoping nobody would ask, "Alex! What's happening with your own art these days?" Hoping none of his students would find him and say, "I'd love to see your paintings sometime." No one ever challenged him in this way, but he feared they would. He'd steer conversations to Flynn Elrod's Minimalism or Billy Al Bengston's latest show. He liked the students but avoided them, with the exception of the few who were so involved in their own work that it didn't matter what Alex was up to. Alex, in fact, liked Gill a lot, except for having to drink his coffee too fast every day.

"What's a good teacher?" Kate asks.

He gets up, starts to paint again. He tells her about classes he's taught, the frustrations and pleasures. She listens, leans against the wall of the garage, asks him more questions. When he can't get any more paint on the canvas, he picks up the dinner tray. She takes the last sip of wine from his glass as they walk to the house.

Sheila, in her room, hears them come in. She's been sitting on her bed for a long time, thinking of Hank, Mac, Ralph. A farewell meditation. She's satisfied. She's said goodbye. From the window, she enjoys the familiar hills. "Home," she thinks, of the banana, plum, summer squash houses whose colors have faded in the evening. It's still early, but she'd like to get a good night's sleep so she can start packing tomorrow. She'll take a quick bath. She unbuttons her blouse. The lights go out in one of the houses. Another house darkens. Then another. She buttons her blouse, grabs her journal, her purse, a sweater. "There are a couple of blankets in Alex's van," she thinks.

164

Kate and Alex sit at the oak table, drinking coffee. How many times has she seen them like this? Kate bends toward Alex, intense about whatever it is she's saying. Alex runs his hand through his hair and nods.

They both look up. Sheila sees in Kate's face the bones of her own face, sees in Alex her own eyes. She puts her arms around Kate, says, "Oh, Mom, I love you."

"I love you, too," Kate says. The three of them move, now—Kate to the stove to put coffee in a thermos for Sheila; Alex to the living room to find the keys to the van where he dropped them on the piano bench; Sheila to the window box where she picks a sprig of parsley and tucks it into a buttonhole of her blouse.

Alex gives her the keys. "We can get along with Kate's car until you've finished moving." He holds her hand tightly.

Sheila gathers her few things, hurries to the van, drives down the hill to Sunset. She steps on the gas as she heads up the ramp of the freeway, takes the freeway to Lincoln Boulevard in Santa Monica, Lincoln south to Venice Boulevard, Venice to her own new street.

The apartment building is an old place, pale aqua stucco with a cluster of palm trees beside the front entrance. Sheila smells salt and fish in the ocean air as she climbs the stairs. "I'm here," she says as she unlocks the door. Her voice echoes. She tries the light switch. The lights come on, just as the landlady said they would. Utilities are included in the rent, like the furniture: a single bed, a desk, a table, two chairs, a small stove and a tiny refrigerator. Sheila puts the thermos on the one kitchen counter, lays her journal on the desk, her sweater and purse and the blankets on the bed.

The apartment is several blocks from the beach, but she can see the ocean during the day from the window over the desk. She can hear it now, she thinks, the constant hiss of tide. She opens the window and puts her head out into the night and shouts, "I'm here!"

She'd planned to sit at the desk and write in her journal, get down her first impressions of her first apartment. But she wants the ocean. She takes off her sandals and rolls up her pants legs, locks the door behind her.

Strange neighborhood. Not safe to be walking alone. Awfully dark, but the young couple that she passes have their arms around each other. A man on one corner calls to his dog, doesn't even glance up as Sheila walks by. She keeps going until she feels sand under her feet. No one is on the beach. Nobody is alive except Sheila and the ocean. She breaks into a run. When she gets the first taste of surf on her toes, she gasps. Cold. Powerful. She wades in up to her knees, shivers with the cold, goes farther. She's dangerously close to being knocked over by the waves, but she can still stand, and does, and begins to sing. Not the blues. Not Laura Nyro songs nor Beethoven's "Ode to Joy." She simply sings, opening her mouth and letting sounds come from her throat until she can hear her voice above the ocean's pounding, until the water grows warm on her legs.

Alex dreams his dream: There is the wall that he had no strength to climb. Now a forceful wind sends him over the barrier, where he lands at the feet of Grandfather Levinsky. The old man is naked, aged, but twice as tall as Alex. The wind lifts Alex and presses him into his grandfather. Alex wants that ancient strength, but just as he begins to merge with it, Grandfather Levinsky rips himself away. "This is the end," he says. Alex reaches to the mythic flesh, crying, "No!" but the huge body, the spirit of his grandfather, disintegrates, particle by particle, until there is nothing left but the grieving wail of the cantor bringing death its proper harmony.

Still dreaming, Alex finds himself in his own kitchen with Kate. She's painting the walls their buttery yellow. He paints with her, but as they paint, the house crumbles under their brushes. When the walls are gone, he discovers himself in another house, an unfinished geometry of air and shadow, where there might be rooms, sometime, but for now the wind that pushed him over the wall blows through it all, chilling him.

In the morning, Alex will wake up, his back aching. He will write the dream, one of the few he's ever taken the trouble to recall completely. The bare new structure of his dream is cold. It's autumn. He has to figure out how to turn on the heat in this place. The solemn music of the cantor moves him, but he understands that he can't listen to that music. There's no time for death now. There's too little time as it is for a forty-five-year-old man. Better to concentrate on the new place. Alex will draw the open beams of the house and fill in the possible walls. He'll cover the gaping air with a ceiling and plan where rooms and windows ought to be. He will come down to earth as he sketches the possibilities, glad, even, for the shock of his separation from the past.

10

AUDREY GIVES HER ROSES a dose of John Elliott's potent aphid killer. She pumps the can energetically, blinks against the echo of spray that comes back to her in the early evening breeze. "I'd better get dressed," she says to the lavender Angel Faces. "You've had enough of this for now." She lingers in the garden, trying not to breathe the poison, but under its metallic odor, the roses' fragrance seduces her into taking one big breath. She cuts a handsome bouquet of the white Honors, then marches to the kitchen where the fragrance shifts from flowers to Audrey's special ham, glazed with honey and mustard, studded with cloves. It sizzles in the oven. "Do your stuff," she encourages it.

She has no control over the ham's tenderness or flavor. "You can't tell by looking at it in the market." She doesn't have any control, either, over the roses, which she arranges carefully in a creamy white ceramic vase. She won't be able to keep them alive past their natural fading, the dropping of petals on the carpet. Audrey can't even control her own body, the feelings she had when John came over with his aphid spray and his martini recipe. As they stood in the kitchen mixing martinis, she wanted to rush to the bathroom for her sea green robe, throw herself on the bed. She didn't. After a couple of drinks, she relaxed enough to carry on a conversation about John's wife—how much he misses the dead woman, though he has to admit that being a bachelor has its advantages. He smiled, lifted his glass to Audrey, silently telling her that she's one reason he's glad to be a widower—sixty-four years old, but still capable of mixing a mean martini and—he hopes—of giving a woman a little pleasure.

Audrey goes into her bedroom to change her clothes, assuring herself that she can keep the romance in check until it's the right time to give in. But she can't. John will appear tonight, "just to see how fast the aphids are dying." "He must have practiced that lopsided grin watching old Gary Cooper movies," Audrey will think, inviting him to join Kate, Alex, Sheila, and herself in their after-dinner talk. John will stay late, much later than the others, and there won't be anything Audrey will be able to do about anything.

She rustles through the summer clothes in her closet. Skirts, blouses, pants, that darling kimono from her birthday. She'll wear that. "White pants, white sleeveless top, the kimono over everything." Shoes. She turns to the long shoe rack. "Ah." The pair of sandals she rarely wears— slender straps woven in black Italian leather—just right to set off the white and the burgundy kimono.

Dressed, she admires herself in the mirror. Her stomach

feels calm. She can eat and drink anything she wants to tonight. There won't be any pain for another few years.

Kate presses the doorbell with one hand, balances a salad bowl in the other. When Audrey opens the door, Kate bubbles, "You look great!" Alex kisses Audrey on the cheek. Sheila gives Audrey a hug and says, "I told Kate that kimono would be perfect for you," pleased that Audrey whispers back, "I love your taste." Sheila's had her hair cut. The wild cluster of brown curls has been sheared to a brief, sculpted cut that makes her face startlingly visible.

"Such bones!" Audrey puts both of her hands on Sheila's face. "You could be a model."

"The haircut's for the nunnery, not for beauty," Sheila jokes.

So it begins, a festive Thursday evening dinner, a gathering of the family. They'll ask themselves what they're celebrating as Audrey passes around the wine, as they eat, as dessert—chocolate mousse—comes victoriously to the table, as John Elliott rings the doorbell.

"My apartment," Sheila thinks, now, before dinner. She celebrated that all last night, and today, packing at Kate and Alex's—box after box of clothes, books, records.

"I might paint in this room," Kate said, tucking scarves and lingerie from the dresser drawers into a box.

. "Fine," Sheila said, thinking that's how it should be—the room transformed into something else, not her bedroom anymore. Not a memory but a whole new idea.

"Have you got any magic spells for leaving home?" Kate asked.

Sheila froze, then saw that Kate was simply pulling

another drawer out of the dresser, hadn't meant to remind her of that night in Berkeley when the vicious power burst through her windows. Maybe they ought to perform a ritual. "I don't remember anything, but we could make one up."

"Earth, water, fire, air," Kate said. "Don't pagans use the four elements in their rituals?"

Kate found chalk in the attic among her paints. Sheila drew a protective circle with it in the middle of the bedroom floor. Kate went to the backyard, dug enough earth to fill a small dish. Sheila found incense. "We've got earth and air," she said. "Water's easy—a bowl of it or anything." She went to the kitchen; Kate got a candle from the living room. "What color?" she called to Sheila. "White," Sheila called back, grabbing a handful of parsley from the window box, then meeting Kate at the stairs.

They set the objects inside the circle, one element for each compass point. Sheila put the parsley in the center. "Natural magic," she said, "depends on herbs. Bonnie used to say that Christ was a magician, born on straw, which is dried grass, an herb. X had a real collection—I don't know what they all were, but they were healing. I know that parsley opens blocked passages in the body, so maybe it will clear out the energy in here."

They stood in the circle and faced the open window, the light that Sheila depended on for years to wake her up, the light that Kate will use for new paintings. "What shall we do?" Kate whispered.

"Say a blessing or something," Sheila said. Kate, stuck for any words of her own, sang "Follow the Gleam," all the way through, every verse. When she stopped, Sheila

171

said the Jewish morning prayer that Grandfather Levinsky had said to her yesterday: "Oh, God, the soul which Thou hast given me is pure," and then, "Powers of the universe, of light and darkness, hear us and bring peace to this room—to its old life and its new life."

After they'd put back the things they'd gathered for the ritual, they started to pack again, neither of them talking. "Anything works if you believe in it," Sheila thought. The room was stacked with boxes. The bed was stripped of sheets. The dresser drawers gaped, empty, in the frame of the dresser.

"Do you want the curtains?" Kate asked.

"No, thanks. I want the ocean air," Sheila had answered. Then she went down to the beauty shop on Sunset to get a haircut.

"I love the ocean air," she says out loud, settled on Audrey's couch with Flower in her lap.

"People are going to the Dead Sea these days for the bromine in the air," Alex tells her. "It heals skin diseases."

"It's the Red Sea," Audrey argues, although she's never heard of bromine or of anybody going to any sea to get it.

"Audrey! I just read an article about it. You don't know what you're talking about!"

"Right," Audrey says, winking at Alex, "but the best place to buy doughnuts is still Mrs. Pearl's on Highland and Melrose."

"That place has been closed for years."

"Right." She makes a quick turn toward the kitchen, giving Alex's arm a squeeze as she goes.

Kate's putting her salad in the refrigerator. "You bought mushrooms? At $1.90 a pound?" Audrey asks.

"We're celebrating," Kate says, hoping Audrey won't ask what they're celebrating. She thinks, "My painting is finished," though its completion is so fresh that she doesn't want to talk about it yet. The woman emerged completely today. "She's alive," Kate had thought. It was done. She turns to the kitchen window. The pink, yellow, white, red and lavender flowers blur in the dusk.

"I'm finally getting rid of the aphids," Audrey says, refilling a half-empty plate of cheesy appetizers.

"Aphids in paradise," Kate murmurs.

Audrey puts a glass of wine in her hand. "You haven't even started drinking."

Kate lifts the glass. "Here's to being kicked out of the Garden of Eden," she says.

"What does that mean?"

"Here's to our last summer."

"You're not getting a divorce!"

"No." Kate looks again at the roses. Once, she would have seen the melting colors as orchids, would have longed for orchids in the greenhouse at home. She's envied Audrey these lush, exquisite flowers and hated her for being such a snob. Thirty rose bushes, for heaven's sake. Tonight she sees, simply, colors merging in the growing darkness and thinks of her finished painting: a woman or Woman searches for her old age, her connection with the future. "Now all I have to do is live it," she thinks.

Alex, in the living room, leans back in his chair, watching Sheila as she sits across from him on the white couch. Her hand moves smoothly over Flower's curved back. How healthy her arms are, bare. Her face in profile is clean, untangled from all that hair. Her cotton dress hangs gracefully from her shoulders to her waist, then drops gently to her calves. "Never be bored with reality," he reminds himself. Reality finds its way into the sore muscle in his back. Middle-aged and out of shape. Well, he's had his chance. God has let him slip by on charm for years. He tries to find Grandfather Levinsky in his mind, but he can't capture the old man's face or voice. "I've never had a real job," he thinks. He yearns for something meaty and substantial to work at. This fall, he'll give himself time to find work that he really can stay with. "How about more wine?" he asks Sheila. She nods, and he heads for the kitchen to celebrate how much his back hurts when he gets out of his comfortable chair. As he reaches the kitchen door, he bumps into Audrey. She's coming through it, carrying the ham to the table in the part of the living room she calls the dining room, although it's only an alcove near the large window on the garden side of the house. She clucks at Alex, so he moves out of her way, then out of Kate's way—she's carrying the salad in one hand and a basket of hot rolls in the other. "Could you get the vegetables?" she asks, and he does—scalloped potatoes and fresh green beans. Sheila, seeing that dinner is under way, goes to the kitchen to bring the wine Alex started to get.

Ready, they stand behind their chairs at the table, waiting for Audrey to signal them to sit. "All of us together," she muses, pleased to have them waiting for her gesture. "Everybody looks nice for once, too," she notices, glad to see Kate in trim black pants and an amber silk blouse. Sheila's wearing one of those Indian print dresses that Audrey considers unbearably ethnic, but she admits it looks wonderful on her—the wide band of—"God! Purple

174

elephants!"—on the full skirt that sets off Sheila's legs. Alex, leaning toward the ham to inhale its aroma, looks handsome, if a little tired. His gray shirt and darker gray slacks satisfy her. "That rabbi must have had an influence on him, sometime." She pulls out her chair and sits down so that everyone else can sit, too.

Kate and Alex's house, in the evening air, is where it has always been: on a hill in Silverlake, where so much touches so much, where the light emphasizes both the similarities and differences of people in the neighborhood. Chicano and Oriental and black and Anglo neighbors wind through the streets in their cars, listening to whatever music they love on their radios. A summer evening, time to relax. The house settles into ground where it's been for sixty years and will be for at least one more generation. The jacaranda tree by the front porch, dropping its flowers, stops in its core. The final blooms loosen and fall. The tree stops not in death, but in turning to the next phase of growth, stops in its wood and sap for a single moment of total rest, then, unseen by anyone, simply begins again in the next moment.

A clean breeze drifts through the house. The stairway, the living room, the study, the kitchen, the bedrooms, are quiet. In the backyard, it's too late for blue jays to feed. The lawn chairs are empty. The greenhouse has nothing to do, which has always been its purpose. In the garage, Alex's painting isn't a painting at all but a series of shadows. Grandfather Levinsky moves through the garage, shaking his head over the painting.

After tonight, he won't come back to the house. "They'll be on their own, and I can stay dead," he mutters, easing through the yard and house to the front porch, where he meets the tree in its moment of pausing. "I want to be dead with God." He feels the tree turn again to life. He doesn't want to be in life but in his own realm until it's time to be born in some other way. "Whatever God chooses," he thinks, without wishing to be a tree, a person, a house, without wishing to be anything except a part of God. He searches for his name, knows he still has it but can't remember it. He can't remember, either, what it's been like to be a man on the earth. He sits on the porch, yet fades, is more and more the gust of wind that anyone passing would see stirring the jacaranda blossoms. The night moves across the neighborhood, and people turn up the music on their car radios against the darkness.

Audrey clears the table. The meat was tender and flavorful. She reminds herself that she wasn't responsible for that. The meat was a blessing. "There must be a God," she thinks, putting leftovers in the refrigerator. She takes a swift look around the kitchen to see if she can get a glimpse of God, but she can't, although she has the sudden sensation of giving up something to the room. "God can take care of it all," she decides as she lifts the chocolate mousse from the refrigerator. It's plump and even-textured. The mousse, too, has been taken care of by God. Audrey and Kate carry it to the table in Audrey's best crystal goblets. "The Holy Grail," Kate says, laughing and setting goblets in front of Alex and Sheila.

"I just didn't have anything smaller," Audrey protests, but the goblets around the table in front of each person do remind her of those old stories of holy pilgrimages, the search for the Grail. Oh, she can't keep that stuff straight—

it gets mixed up with Bible stories of blind men seeing, of fish and bread multiplying.

When the doorbell rings, it's John, followed by Ming, who rushes to Audrey, meowing for praise at his good sense in finding John at the door. "Hello, hello," Audrey says, waving him to a place at the table as Alex pulls up a chair for him. "So, how fast are the aphids dying?" John asks, grinning at Audrey. Alex and Kate and Sheila smile knowingly at each other. Kate gets up to take care of the kitchen mess before the three of them embarrass John. Let Audrey enjoy this.

She fills the sink with soapy water. Audrey won't want to put her precious china in the dishwasher. She washes the dishes slowly as she listens with half an ear to the living room conversation. Lots of chatter about aphids, about the neighborhood. Then Sheila describes her new place. Kate hears John grunt appreciatively. "Youngsters should be on their own," he pronounces. "Why, when my girl was your age—" Kate feels the God that Audrey felt here in the kitchen, taking care of things tonight. Then she feels something else—the cool air of the future. Sam will die in the next few months. She'll face her classes of art students and be shocked at how much her voice will echo Sam's when she talks about the inevitable line.

The multiple gods of the city. Some are pushing Kate to her own conclusion, which will bring her the challenge to live everything before she dies, years from now. She'll be close to her first grandchild with his wise, Grandfather Levinsky face. Eventually, she'll help pay for his education with the money she'll make as an old woman, money from her paintings. Her place in the outer world of art that she's about to enter will pay to send an odd little boy through college, then law school—his choice. Kate will see that as a waste of his spiritual nature, but she'll do it, loving the boy as much as she understands her own mother loves her. She hears Audrey say to Sheila, "If there's anything you need for your place, let me know. How about a set of dishes? I'll bet you're eating off an old cracked plate and have one lousy cup for coffee—how about a set of coffee mugs—really nice ones without any corny sayings or pictures of pigs and cows on them? Listen, when your parents were first married, you should have seen the junk they had—no, I shouldn't say junk—it was all artistic, handmade ceramic bowls and cups—but I always thought I'd get lead poisoning eating out of those crazy clay things."

After Alex dies, Kate will sell the house. She'll have an apartment of her own, still in the fertile light of the Silverlake hills. It will be a small place. Living close to herself will bring her great pleasure and great loneliness. She will end her life doing precise drawings of loneliness, never turning that demon into an angel, but offering herself to it, ripening in the loneliness as the wheat that lives in the gold of her hair ripens toward harvest.

It was a good dinner, a fine celebration. It's dark outside. The roses have disappeared. Kate hears a lull in the conversation, so wipes her hands, walks to the doorway. "It's time to go," she says.

178